MAHENDRA JAPE

INITIATED BY AI

Who Decides Now?

London

First published by Owlia Publishing House, London 2026

Copyright © 2026 by Mahendra Jape

All rights reserved. No part of this publication may be reproduced, stored, or transmitted in any form or by any means, electronic, mechanical, photocopying, recording, scanning, or otherwise without written permission from the publisher. It is illegal to copy this book, post it to a website, or distribute it by any other means without permission.

Mahendra Jape asserts the moral right to be identified as the author of this work.

Mahendra Jape has no responsibility for the persistence or accuracy of URLs for external or third-party Internet Websites referred to in this publication and does not guarantee that any content on such Websites is, or will remain, accurate or appropriate.

Designations used by companies to distinguish their products are often claimed as trademarks. All brand names and product names used in this book and on its cover are trade names, service marks, trademarks, and registered trademarks of their respective owners. The publishers and the book are not associated with any product or vendor mentioned in this book. None of the companies referenced within the book have endorsed the book.

This book features stories and examples drawn from research, interviews, and public sources. When individuals are described, these are composite characters based on multiple sources. Specific details, locations, institutions, and circumstances have been modified to protect privacy and confidentiality. The scenarios depicted reflect patterns observed across various organisations and sectors, not failures at any particular institution.

The structural dynamics they experience are documented patterns rather than isolated incidents.

This book is for informational purposes only and does not constitute legal, medical, or professional advice. The Golem legend (Jewish folklore) and Chakravyuha (Hindu Mahabharata) are used in this book as metaphors for analysing patterns in AI systems. These references are illustrative and not meant as commentary on or representation of any religious tradition or community. The interpretations are conceptual tools to understand technological dynamics, not religious or cultural statements.

While every effort has been made to ensure accuracy, the information in this book is provided "as is" without warranty of any kind. The author shall not be liable for any damages resulting from the use of this information.

Book cover design © 2026 by Mahendra Jape

First edition

ISBN: 978-1-9195202-0-9

*This book was professionally typeset on Reedsy.
Find out more at reedsy.com*

This book is dedicated to my parents.

My father, a firefighter, maintained throughout his career that fire serves or destroys, depending on how it is governed. He understood that the most formidable forces demand the most vigilant stewardship.

My mother, a teacher, devoted her professional life to preparing students for futures she could scarcely envision. She held that education ought to cultivate independent thought rather than mere compliance with instruction.

Contents

Preface ii
Acknowledgments v
About the Author vii
1 THE FIRST MOVE 1
2 THE ARRANGED WORLD 15
3 RELATIONAL POSITIONING 25
4 THE AGE OF ELSEWHERE 35
5 THE GROUND WE STAND ON 41
6 THE LOGIC OF CONTEXT BLINDNESS 47
7 THE TRAPS CLOSE 55
8 PRISONERS OF PROGRESS 69
9 HINGE 75
10 SURFING THE TRANSITION 77
11 BUILDING COGNITIVE CAPABILITY 83
12 THE RIGHT TO THINK 91
13 THE STRUCTURES OF INFLUENCE 99
14 HUMAN ACCOUNTABILITY 109
15 WHAT REMAINS HUMAN 119
16 EPILOGUE FOR MANAGEMENT 133
Notes on Sources 139
Further Reading 151
Index 160

Preface

Intelligence began before language.

Long before people explained the world, survival depended on noticing signals that appeared without warning. A rustle in the grass. A sudden quiet in the trees. An unfamiliar call overhead. These signs did not explain themselves. Those who noticed them in time lived long enough to learn what they meant.

In parts of the Indian subcontinent, hunters learnt that the Rufous Treepie often reacted before a tiger became visible. Its alarm call became information. Hear the bird and expect a predator. In northern Tanzania, honey hunters worked with the honeyguide, a bird that led them to hives it could not open. What appeared to be instinct was attention shaped by experience. Repeated signals turned into guidance. Something appears. You respond. Only later do you understand.

This sequence still governs human behaviour. Detection comes first. Understanding follows. Much of what we call judgement begins as a response to something that stands out.

Today, the signals no longer come from forests or fields. They appear on screens. Prompts, rankings, highlights, recommendations. Before you finish typing a search, suggestions appear. You choose one because it is close enough to what you meant. The suggestion arrives before the intention.

To understand Artificial Intelligence (AI), it is helpful to set aside the idea that it is a mind inside a machine. These systems do not think or understand in the human sense. They learn from examples, extract regularities, and produce outputs that resemble answers. The resemblance is convincing because it is fluent and fast.

The difficulty is not that machines behave without understanding. The difficulty is that behaviour which looks intelligent invites trust. Trust removes hesitation. Once hesitation fades, outputs begin to guide action quietly. What feels like assistance begins to shape where attention starts, what options seem relevant, and what gets ignored.

AI is often described as a tool, and tools are often left unclaimed. A hammer sits in a drawer until it is picked up. A calculator waits until it is opened. The tool does nothing until a human decides to use it. It has neither agenda nor initiative. AI systems, however, do something more than that. They prepare the environment in which choices are made. A playlist is already queued. Routes appear before you think about the journey. Your email client suggests how to finish a sentence you have not yet decided to write.

When the starting point of thought shifts, everything that follows shifts with it. The question is not whether machines will replace people. The question is: what happens when the first step of thinking occurs elsewhere, and people begin from there?

* * *

Before the arguments begin, meet three people. Sarah reads medical scans for a living and has recently noticed something unsettling about how she begins each examination. Marcus holds his engineering team together in ways that never appear in performance reviews. Aisha is still trying to get in the door. You will follow all three through this book, and by the end, you will understand why their situations are not separate problems but one problem seen from different angles. The book moves in three stages: the shift, the lock-in, and what remains, and it builds deliberately. If the early chapters feel dense, that density is the point. What is being described is a structure that is hard to see precisely because it arrived quietly, one reasonable decision at a time.

Acknowledgments

To the many who contributed ideas, challenges, and the occasional well-timed scepticism: some of you asked not to be named, and the rest of you probably should have. You know who you are, and so, apparently, does the AI.

To Priti, thank you for your patience while I stared blankly at the walls for four months, and for gently reminding me that 'AI will initiate' was not a valid excuse for forgetting to take out the bins.

To Nau, who provided the necessary reality check every time I started taking myself too seriously. Thank you for reminding me that while AI might be able to pass the Turing test, it still could not explain why the Wi-Fi went down the moment you started playing games online.

To Tanu, now at Cornell, thank you for calling at exactly the right moments and never the wrong ones. Whether challenging my ideas from the corridor of our mansion or interrogating them from Ithaca, your check-ins kept me honest.

To Shilpa, my most honest, if somewhat unwilling, beta reader. Your reluctance was the perfect stress test for this manuscript. When you finished it without falling asleep, I considered it a triumph for humanity.

To my dear brother Kedar. You have read so many drafts that you have essentially become an AI expert against your will. I apologise for the involuntary career change; any remaining errors are mine.

And finally, to my laptop. Thank you for not becoming sentient and deleting this manuscript during the sixty-third draft. I promise to keep your fans clean and your battery charged as a token of my gratitude.

About the Author

Mahendra Jape is a trusted strategic adviser to multinational corporations and technology firms navigating the complexities of AI implementation and data strategy. Over two decades, he has worked at the intersection of automation, organisational change, and regulatory risk, specialising in structural transformations whose full impact emerges only months and years after systems are operational and institutional dependencies have locked in.

His work addresses questions most organisations find hard to confront: how automation redistributes expertise, where change management frameworks break down under real-world conditions, and how regulatory exposure compounds as AI systems become embedded in critical workflows.

Initiated by AI argues that most organisations are responding to structural pressures rather than making strategic choices about AI. The book shows how tools that solve immediate problems create dependencies that narrow future options and close the trap through success rather than failure.

The book equips leaders to recognise these dynamics before lock-in occurs and to understand what must be actively preserved for human judgement to survive the transition.

Mahendra works with leaders at the point where strategy meets consequence.

1

THE FIRST MOVE

Sarah Patel knew something was wrong before she could name it. The CT scan appeared on her screen at 11.45 am, but the AI overlay had not loaded yet. No red boxes appeared around suspicious regions. No confidence scores lined the sidebar. Just the raw image, waiting to be reviewed. Sarah stared at the scan, her cursor hovering somewhere near the centre. For the first time in months, she did not immediately know where to begin.

Three seconds passed. Then four. When the overlay finally returned, red boxes appeared around a small nodule in the upper left quadrant with a high confidence score, and her eyes went exactly where the software directed. She completed the report in twenty-eight minutes, well within her throughput target, and the workflow continued as if nothing had happened.

Sarah had been reading scans for twelve years. Medical school taught her anatomy, and residency taught her pathology, but the real education came later. It came in the thousands of images where experience settled into instinct, where she learnt to notice the irregular borders and subtle changes in density. These patterns refused to resolve cleanly. This way of seeing did not translate into words or instructions. It formed through repetition, through case reviews, through years of confronting ambiguity until her eyes knew where to move before conscious analysis began.

She had once spent twenty-five minutes on a scan that appeared completely normal. Something kept pulling her attention back to the upper left quadrant, a discomfort she could not articulate but could not ignore. The tumour was there when she finally found it, three millimetres across, still in its earliest stage. The software, when tested later on the same image, returned a result of 'insufficient data'. Sarah had not worked through a checklist to find it. She had entered the image and knew where to look.

Sarah, before the use of overlays, understood how her own attention moved through an examination. Sarah, after the use of overlays, waited for the boxes to indicate where to start.

The overlay was implemented as a routine software update two years earlier, presented as a form of assistance. In practice, it shaped control. Rectangular markers appeared on the scan viewer, highlighting areas of concern with confidence scores displayed beside them. Colleagues talked about improved accuracy. Administrators talked about faster throughput. Everyone agreed it was a valuable tool, something that would make the work easier and the outcomes better.

Digital systems had organised Sarah's workflow for years. PACS, the hospital's imaging archive and viewing system, worked alongside the radiology work-list to prioritise urgent cases. Protocols determined which sequences to run. These systems arranged the order in which scans arrived. They did not tell Sarah where to look once an image appeared on her screen. The overlay crossed that line. It determined where her examination would begin within each scan, marking regions of interest before she had seen anything herself.

Sarah treated the overlay as a reference point. She would read a scan in her own way, following the patterns her training had built, and then compare her findings with the software's highlights. Sometimes the markers pointed to areas she had noted. Sometimes they drew attention to regions she would have examined anyway. The alignment between her judgement and the software's suggestions grew steadily stronger. Comparison became confirmation, and confirmation settled into habit.

One day in October, though she could not say which day, the sequence reversed. She no longer read the scan first. She began with the boxes and built her examination from there. The software determined where she looked, and she decided what to do about what she found there.

That distinction still mattered. Her name went on every report. She was still the doctor. Her judgement was still required for the diagnosis to be complete. But the examination itself no longer began with her. The first move now belonged to the machine.

What Machines Can See

Around the same time, a second and distinct system was being piloted at hospitals across the network. Where the CT overlay directed Sarah's attention within individual scans, this one operated at a different scale entirely. A diagnostic algorithm trained on more than 2 million mammograms, validated across 43 institutions in 14 countries, had been running in clinical evaluation sites where it assessed risk years before visible tumours appeared. The system analysed patterns invisible to the human eye and produced personalised risk scores that predicted which patients would develop breast cancer within five years.

The technology identified high-risk patients with nearly twice the accuracy of traditional clinical models. Where established risk assessment tools correctly flagged 23% of women who would develop cancer within five years, the algorithm identified 41%. The difference translated into lives saved by earlier intervention, before the disease advanced beyond the point of treatment.

What distinguished this system was its capacity to detect signals radiologists could not see. A mammogram that appeared entirely normal to trained human eyes contained information that the algorithm recognised as predictive. Tissue patterns, density distributions, and subtle asymmetries that fell below the threshold of human perception coalesced into risk profiles that the software quantified with precision. The model performed consistently across patient populations that varied by age, ethnicity, and breast density, maintaining performance in Sweden, Taiwan, Brazil, Israel, and the United States without requiring adjustment for local conditions.

Sarah attended the departmental briefing where the administration explained the research partnership. The hospital had joined an international evaluation network, one of a small number of early clinical sites testing whether the algorithm could function reliably outside controlled research conditions. The algorithm would run in parallel with standard diagnostic review, flagging patients whose scans suggested elevated risk even when current images showed no abnormalities. Those patients would receive enhanced screening protocols, closer monitoring intervals, and earlier access to preventive interventions. The programme aimed to shift cancer detection upstream, identifying disease before symptoms appeared and prognosis narrowed.

The presentation included validation data that Sarah found difficult to ignore. The system had been validated on more than 1.5 million mammograms. Performance remained stable across diverse populations, suggesting the technology would function reliably regardless of where patients lived or their demographic category. The model identified patterns that predicted cancer development three, four, even five years before diagnosis, operating at temporal scales human assessment could not match.

The briefing did not address how the technology would reshape Sarah's professional identity. The algorithm could already see further into the future than she could. It detected risks she would miss, identified patients she would clear, and stratified populations with granularity her clinical training had not equipped her to achieve. Her diagnostic skill remained necessary to interpret visible abnormalities, but risk assessment had moved beyond the threshold at which human perception functioned reliably.

She understood the clinical value. Patients flagged as high-risk could begin surveillance before cancer developed, when intervention offered the greatest chance of survival. Earlier detection led to less aggressive treatment, better outcomes, and longer survival. The evidence supported adoption, and the algorithm delivered results no human-based system could replicate.

Yet something fundamental had shifted. The technology did not assist her risk assessment. It performed a function she had never been able to perform, identifying patterns that remained invisible even when she knew where to look. The algorithm operated in a domain beyond human expertise, and the gap between what the system perceived and what she could see widened with each model iteration.

The hospital formally joined the evaluation network three months after the briefing. Sarah's workflow remained unchanged in procedural terms. She reviewed scans, identified abnormalities, and wrote reports. The algorithm ran alongside her, processing the same images and producing risk scores that appeared in a separate field of the diagnostic interface. High-risk classifications triggered protocols for enhanced screening and specialist referral. The system executed its function independently of Sarah's assessment, operating on information she could not access, even when the same image sat before her.

One afternoon, she reviewed a screening mammogram that appeared entirely normal. Tissue density within expected parameters, no masses, no calcifications, no architectural distortion. She cleared the patient for routine annual follow-up and closed the report. The algorithm flagged the same scan as high-risk, projecting a high probability of cancer development within three years. Sarah reopened the image and examined it again, searching for whatever the system had detected. Nothing appeared abnormal. The tissue looked healthy, the patterns unremarkable, the scan indistinguishable from thousands of others she had cleared without concern.

She approved the high-risk classification, and the patient was placed under enhanced surveillance. Eighteen months later, a follow-up scan revealed early-stage ductal carcinoma, small enough that treatment remained minimally invasive and prognosis stayed favourable. The algorithm had been correct. Sarah had been wrong, though calling it wrong felt imprecise. She had read the scan accurately in accordance with all the standards her training recognised. The cancer had not been visible. By the time she reviewed the image, the technology had already detected something else. Not the tumour, which had not yet formed, but the conditions that would produce it. It identified correlations between tissue structure and density that predicted future malignancy even when conventional pathology was absent. The system operated at a pattern-recognition level that exceeded the resolving limits of human expert judgement.

Sarah knew she ought to feel grateful. The cancer had been identified early enough that treatment would likely spare the patient from the harms of late intervention. The system had behaved exactly as intended, flagging risk before disease became visible and enabling action that would probably save a life.

What she felt instead was a loss of footing. Her expertise still mattered when pathology was present. It mattered less once assessment shifted from reading what existed to anticipating what would emerge. She had trained herself to notice subtle cues in images. The algorithm drew on signals that did not present themselves as images at all, extracting meaning from relationships that never reached conscious perception.

The distinction mattered because it was categorical rather than incremental. No additional training could move her into the domain in which the system operated. What confronted her was not a more capable practitioner working within the same frame, but a different mode of assessment that redefined what diagnostic judgement could reach.

Technology would continue to advance. With each iteration,

it absorbed more cases, more outcomes, and longer temporal sequences. Its perceptual range would expand, while hers would remain bound by biology. The gap would widen, and her role would contract into the residual space the system could not yet occupy, until even that space narrowed enough for her presence to shift from necessary to optional.

She finished her shift and walked to the car park, the successful early detection still sitting uncomfortably in her thoughts. The patient would live. The system had worked. The future it represented was already here, operating in parallel with her work, quietly demonstrating that human expertise had reached the limits of what perception alone could achieve.

The question was not whether the technology should be adopted. The clinical evidence made that decision inevitable. The question was: what remained human when machines could see the future more clearly than the people responsible for deciding how to respond?

When Assistance Becomes Necessity

Sarah was not made redundant. Her salary did not decrease. Her measurable productivity improved. The hospital tracked throughput, and by every metric that mattered to administration, the numbers looked better than before. More scans were processed per shift. Fewer cases required extended review. Diagnostic consistency improved across the department, and the backlog was reduced.

She could not say when the change in how she began each examination had occurred. One afternoon, several months later, the software loaded more slowly than usual. The scan appeared on Sarah's screen without the familiar overlays. She paused, her cursor drifting near the edge of the viewing area as she searched for the visual cues that usually arrived first. The image was complete and readable, yet her examination felt incomplete without the red boxes that usually anchored her attention.

A colleague passed behind her workstation and glanced at the screen. 'Waiting for the overlay?' he asked, a hint of recognition in his voice that suggested he had felt the same hesitation himself.

Sarah nodded and looked back at the image, trying to recover the sense of orientation she remembered having years before, when every scan began as unmarked territory, and her attention moved through it according to patterns she had spent years developing. The feeling did not return easily. She could read the scan, certainly. She still knew what she was looking at. But the starting point, the place where her examination would naturally begin, felt uncertain without the guidance she had learnt to expect.

The delay lasted only a few seconds, after which the markers reappeared, and her work resumed its normal rhythm. But the moment stayed with her. Something fundamental had shifted in how she approached her work, though she could not pinpoint exactly when the change had occurred. Her reading followed whatever the software decided to show her first.

Eleven months after the overlay first arrived, Sarah's hospital introduced a new initiative. Radiologists were asked to help train the next version of the diagnostic system by flagging cases in which their clinical judgement disagreed with the automated markers. The request seemed reasonable, a means to refine the technology and improve its accuracy. Sarah opened the new interface to review the instructions. The rectangles were there, highlighting regions before she had looked at anything. She noticed a toggle in the corner of the screen, an option to turn off the overlay entirely if she preferred to work without it.

The option existed, but using it felt impossible. She toggled it off once. The unmarked scan looked the same as it always had, but she could not immediately decide where to begin. She toggled it back on, and the boxes returned, along with the certainty of knowing where to look.

Sarah realised she had forgotten how her eyes used to move through a scan before the boxes appeared to guide them.

The Ordered List

Hiring followed the same logic, though it arrived in stages and felt more justifiable at each step. A recruiter once began their work by reading an application. They would notice something in the way a candidate described their experience, or spot a detail that suggested real competence, or see a gap in the timeline that deserved explanation before forming any conclusions. Evaluation began with human attention, making deliberate choices about where to look and what to prioritise. The process was subjective, yet responsive to context in ways formal criteria could not easily capture.

Hiring moved online, and the number of applications for any given position began to increase dramatically. What had once been a manageable stack of printed CVs became a queue of hundreds of digital files, far more than any single person could read carefully in the allocated hours. New software was introduced to manage the overwhelming flow. Early versions grouped candidates by basic criteria such as education level or years of experience. Recruiters still read applications, but someone else's algorithm had decided the order in which they encountered them.

Later iterations made ranking a priority. Candidates were ranked, with those at the top identified as most promising by weighted formulae that compared keywords, credentials, and prior hiring outcomes. Shortlists had already formed before any human being looked at a name or read a description of someone's work history. These tools were adopted to address scale and ease pressure on decision-makers, and they worked exactly as intended.

A hiring manager would open the talent management app and begin with whoever appeared at the top of the list. Interviews followed that order. Discussion and approval still occurred; the hiring team still met to compare notes, but the path towards a hiring decision had narrowed considerably before any substantive conversation with a candidate. Selection was underway before evaluation had formally begun.

The role remained open for months, so the recruiter reopened the list of rejected candidates. One application revealed the timing of the filtering. A single-letter typo, "manger" instead of "manager", had excluded a candidate with eight years of operations experience. The system had filtered the application out instantly.

Decisions about whom to hire still formally belonged to human beings. The ordering that determined which candidates would ever be seriously considered, however, belonged to the machine. People still made the final decision, but only after the algorithm had identified the options worth choosing from. The apparatus still required human judgement, but the opening move was no longer theirs to make.

Three Hundred Thousand Years

For most of human history, the beginning of work was a human decision. People noticed something, judged that it mattered, and then acted on that judgement. Tools and techniques were subsequently used to support the decision. A farmer decided which field to plough and then reached for the appropriate tool. A craftsman decided what to build and then selected materials accordingly. The sequence always began with human intention, and everything else served that initial act of noticing and deciding.

This arrangement started to shift long before AI entered the picture. People began leaving marks in sand to hold memories outside their own minds, externalising what they might otherwise forget. They drew maps rather than relying entirely on landmarks and local knowledge, capturing spatial relationships on paper for later consultation. They wrote down instructions rather than transmitting expertise through speech and demonstration, creating records that could endure beyond the immediate presence of the person who knew how to do something.

Each of these steps pushed the starting point further from immediate human choice. But historically, technology waited to be used. Now it acts first.

AI accelerates this shift beyond what previous technologies achieved. It acts in advance, supplying the starting point directly, often before you have consciously formed an intention of your own.

Sarah's diagnostic overlay tells her where the reading should begin, which regions deserve attention first and which can be examined later. The hiring algorithm tells recruiters which candidates are worth evaluating in the first place, shaping the pool before assessment starts. Your email agent makes that determination on your behalf and then asks you to confirm or adjust its decisions within the structure it has created.

When tools waited for humans to provide direction, expertise meant knowing when to start looking and where to direct attention first. When tools begin acting before humans do, expertise shifts towards knowing how to respond appropriately to decisions.

And here is what makes this particular moment in the history of technology different from every previous wave: the starting point is the most valuable part of any process. Whoever frames the question exercises significant control over what kinds of answers are possible. The person who decides where attention should be directed controls, to a considerable degree, what is actually seen and what remains in the background. Whoever sets the agenda for a meeting shapes the conversation before a single word is spoken. The person who makes the first move in any strategic situation establishes the context within which all subsequent moves must be made.

This is precisely the position that AI algorithms have now claimed. They make the first move, and humans respond. Once the initial position is taken, the terms are set, and the frame is established, everything that follows is a response. It may be a skilled response, carefully considered and competently executed. But it is a response nonetheless, an action that occurs within boundaries drawn by someone or something else.

Authority Relocated

Sarah still reads scans every day. The recruiter continues to evaluate candidates and make hiring decisions. You still review your email and decide which messages warrant a reply. Work continues as usual, and professionals remain responsible. Expertise still shapes outcomes.

But the examination now begins wherever the machine has decided to point and anchor attention. The candidate shortlist now begins with the highest-ranked candidate by the algorithm. Your day starts with the items your interfaces flag as important or urgent. The frame arrives before you do, and your skill works within it rather than creating it.

It is a question of who or what arrives first. And in the economy that is forming around these technologies, arriving first matters more than almost anything else. Arriving first means you get to set the terms of engagement. Setting the terms means you determine what will count as real, what will be recognised as deserving attention, and what will stay entirely outside the frame.

For three hundred thousand years, humans decided when work began. That has now changed. The machine is set to arrive first.

2

THE ARRANGED WORLD

What happened to Sarah in the radiology department did not stay there.

A project manager opened her calendar on Monday morning. Three meetings had appeared over the weekend, pulled from email threads she had been copied on by an AI agent. Each had a time, a participant list, and agenda bullets extracted from the messages. None had been confirmed, yet they sat there as if they had. Declining meant doing nothing, and accepting meant clicking once. By the time she finished her coffee, her week had been shaped by decisions she had not made. Whatever action she eventually took, the AI agent had already influenced her thinking by determining which conversations would take place and when they would occur.

This is where the previous chapter left us. Sarah's examination began at the point indicated by the overlay. The project manager's week began wherever the agent decided. The sequence was already in place before either of them arrived to work within it.

What follows is the same logic operating at two different

levels. The first is the level of sequence, who arranges the order in which things appear. The second is the level of framing, who determines what appears at all.

Together, they answer a question raised in the previous chapter but not fully resolved. It is not just that AI acts first. It is that by acting first, it decides what you will see, what you will consider, and what will never reach you at all.

When Solutions Relocate Decisions

A woman stood in her kitchen on a Sunday afternoon, unpacking shopping bags, when she realised she had forgotten the cooking oil. It was still sitting on the supermarket shelf. She had walked past the aisle twice. The item had been on her mental list when she left the house, clear enough that she had not written it down. Somewhere between the entrance and the checkout, she had forgotten.

She reached for her phone and added cooking oil to the supermarket loyalty app, flagging it for next time. Then she added the other items she kept forgetting. Sugar. Rice. Salt. Onions. The app promised to remember these patterns and surface them when needed. It seemed practical. A solution to a problem she had been managing badly.

Six months later, she opened the app on Saturday morning and found her basket already populated. Twelve items were awaiting approval, selected from patterns tracked by the loyalty programme since she began relying on it. Bread appeared every Thursday. Coffee arrived when the previous bag should have been running low. The meal kit she had ordered twice in December was now appearing weekly, even though it was flagged as a preference she had not consciously set.

Now the noticing happened elsewhere. The app tracked buying habits and surfaced items when algorithms judged the household was running low. She reviewed the suggestions, removed what seemed excessive, and added what the programme had missed. Her role had narrowed to verification.

The shift had felt helpful throughout. It still saved hours and reduced the mental effort required to remember staples. The app had learnt patterns she had not intended to establish as permanent. The chocolate bar purchased on three consecutive Saturdays became a weekly recommendation. The premium coffee, once bought as a treat, became the default. Small indulgences converted into expected purchases simply through repetition, and the algorithm reinforced what had started as exceptions.

She tried declining the suggestions. The items reappeared the following week, rising higher in the list through personalised promotions that were hard to ignore. Repeatedly declining required more effort than accepting once, and carried the sense that the offer might be missed. The path of least effort ran through approval.

Spending had climbed without an obvious cause, eighteen per cent higher than the previous year, spread across hundreds of small approvals that felt reasonable individually. The app was optimised for engagement. Personalised suggestions drove higher transaction frequency. Convenience for her meant revenue for the platform, and the two interests had aligned until they diverged.

She deleted the app one Sunday and went to the shop without it. She stood in the cleaning products aisle, trying to remember which brand she usually bought, whether the larger size was a good value, and how much was left at home. The questions appeared more difficult than they should have been. Decisions that once took seconds stretched into minutes of uncertainty. She had stopped carrying those details in her head because the app had been carrying them for her.

She reinstalled the app immediately after reaching home. The cognitive work of household supplies had been outsourced long enough that retrieving them felt like relearning from the beginning. The app had made her faster by making her dependent, and the dependency revealed itself only when she tried to function without it.

The app suggested it, and she kept approving. The system functioned, goods arrived, and the household ran. But she had not asked herself what was now deciding what she really needed.

Navigation makes the pattern clearer. A route appears the moment a destination is entered. Before you have moved, the path is already selected. Turn-by-turn directions guide each step, and the journey succeeds without spatial understanding. You reach the destination but cannot retrace the route without help. The system handled thinking that you once did.

A driver entered an unfamiliar area outside Bristol, following GPS directions. The route was adjusted for traffic and delays. Instructions appeared, and the car moved forward smoothly. Partway through the journey, the screen froze.

The road was still there, and the vehicle could still move. The driver slowed and pulled towards the kerb, waiting for the route to recalculate. Landmarks offered little help because navigation had turned conditional on the signal.

Evaluation After Selection

Organisations track throughput, completion rates, error counts, and similar indicators. These numbers begin to define what is perceived as real when decisions are made. Aspects that shape long-term outcomes but cannot be measured daily are harder to detect. They still shape outcomes, but they do not appear in the data people examine when deciding what to do next.

A logistics depot manager described the problem in practical terms. His warehouse tracked pick rates, pack rates, accuracy scores, and dispatch times. The dashboard updated every fifteen minutes. Performance reviews compared individuals against team averages. The system identified inefficiencies with precision.

What it could not capture was why the most experienced workers sometimes moved more slowly than newer staff. The veterans knew which products were fragile, which boxes needed reinforcement, and which customers always complained when items arrived in certain configurations. They worked around problems that would only surface days later, after the package had travelled and the customer had opened it. Their knowledge remained latent, preventing escalations that would cost far more than the seconds lost during packing.

The dashboard treated their caution as inefficiency. Managers received regular prompts to address underperformance. The experienced workers either accelerated to meet the metrics or left for roles in which their judgement was valued. When that happened, the return rates climbed. The warehouse hired more staff to handle the surge in problem resolution.

Each preconfigured choice seems minor. Together they alter how people relate to their own work, not by replacing them, but by determining the conditions under which their judgement is exercised.

The junior doctor opened the discharge summary and felt the ground shift under the job. The document was written, complete enough to sign, with the right headings, the right tone, and the tidy certainty that makes a hospital record look complete.

It contained the diagnosis, treatment plan, and follow-up instructions, arranged under familiar headings, as if composed by someone who had been present throughout the entire admission alongside the patient.

The doctor had not typed a word. A programme had pulled fragments from scattered notes, test results, triage entries, and abbreviations buried across the electronic health record. It assembled them into a coherent clinical narrative. The doctor read it as one reads a statement that bears one's name before agreeing with its meaning.

One sentence suggested the wrong emphasis. A risk section lacked crucial context about the patient's living situation. A follow-up instruction could easily be misread by someone unfamiliar with the case. The doctor corrected what mattered most, deleted what was misleading, added a clarification to prevent confusion later, and signed.

From the hospital's perspective, nothing had changed. A clinician reviewed the discharge summary and was accountable. The process completed smoothly. The institution absorbed the moment without noticing any shift.

But something essential had moved earlier in the sequence. The programme had decided what mattered before the doctor began reading.

Framing Before Choice

You walk into a restaurant, sit at a table, and look at the menu. The menu offers choice, but it also defines the boundaries within which that choice can occur. You compare dishes, weigh prices against your hunger, consider dietary restrictions, and decide what to order. Yet you choose only among options that the kitchen can prepare, the supply chain can deliver, and the business model can support profitably. Dishes that are not on the menu rarely enter your mind as possibilities, even though the ingredients may exist in the kitchen and the chef may know how to prepare them. The menu shapes your choice by determining what is available before you sit down.

AI functions similarly in work environments. When options appear on a dashboard, when alternatives have been filtered and formatted for review, the field of possibility has been drawn. The professional evaluates what appears, but what appears has already been selected and anchored. Candidates below certain thresholds are excluded before consideration begins and never enter the review process.

The manager still decides whom to hire, but the pool of candidates was determined by software that applied rules the manager may not fully understand and did not design.

Signal and Noise

Situations are compressed into data points that can be disseminated throughout the organisation and reach the people responsible for decision-making. Once that compression becomes routine, selection appears less like an active choice. It feels procedural, as if things have always worked this way.

Some features of a situation become legible signals that the AI system can compare and act on. Other features remain, but they fall outside the system's frame for organising information. The distinction appears neutral, but it is not a difference between information and absence. There is a difference between what the system treats as signal and what it sidelines as noise, even when those sidelined elements still shape outcomes.

Hospitals have always collected data. What AI systems do is determine which data points matter, surfacing some as signals worth acting on and pushing others into the background. Waiting times, scan volumes, readmission rates, and protocol compliance scores become the visible reality of the organisation, not because they are the most important measures, but because they are the ones AI systems can process and rank.

The hardest parts to capture, often those that matter most to actual outcomes, elude this kind of measurement. Whether a patient truly understood the discharge plan and felt capable of following it at home. Whether pain was managed effectively in the weeks following a procedure. Whether the family was prepared for what recovery would actually require. These realities continue to shape what happens next, yet they do not move within the organisation in a way that allows them to be treated as signals.

Sarah encountered this logic in her daily practice. An older patient presented with symptoms that had developed slowly over several weeks. No single test captured the full picture. Multiple areas seemed involved, including subtle changes in memory, intermittent weakness in one arm, unexplained weight loss, and persistent low-grade pain. The pattern did not fit cleanly into any standard diagnostic pathway.

Defending the hours required to work within that uncertainty meant translating concern into terms the hospital recognised. Patient care continues; the case has not been discharged. But the justification weakens when it cannot be expressed in codes, scores, or adherence to the institution's formalised pathways.

The same constraint shapes how AI systems are developed. Emphasis tends to fall on features that present as clear, repeatable patterns in the data. That constraint does not stay inside the organisation. It shapes the signals that the next generation of AI systems is built to recognise.

Ranked Before Seen

Items placed higher in a sequence gain significance through position alone, before any human evaluates them. Every ordered list rests on earlier choices about what to include, how to weight different factors, and which criteria to treat as decisive. Those choices announce themselves as rankings, highlights, and recommendations. What disappears is the memory that they were choices at all.

Hiring algorithms compound this. A system trained on ten years of employment records learns that graduates from certain universities receive offers more frequently. The pattern exists because earlier hiring managers favoured those institutions. The algorithm treats the correlation as a signal and amplifies it. Future candidates from those universities rank higher. The bias that began as a human preference becomes a feature of the system, and the system's outputs become the training data for the next iteration.

What began as a design choice starts to feel like common sense. Alternatives lose standing because they occur less frequently and become increasingly difficult to defend against frameworks widely adopted within the organisation. When someone wants to challenge the setup, the field of acceptable debate has already been set by earlier choices that no longer register as choices, because they are embedded in the infrastructure everyone uses to coordinate their work.

The junior doctor signed the discharge summary. The boxes were ticked. The patient would leave with instructions that looked complete. But the starting point had been chosen before the doctor arrived, and the gaps that remained would only show themselves later, in ways the system was not built to see.

What systems cannot measure, they cannot protect. That includes people.

3

RELATIONAL POSITIONING

Marcus Tropos read the restructuring email twice. The firm was reducing the engineering division by 30%. Performance metrics would determine who stayed. Lines of code written, features shipped, bugs closed, velocity scores. The language was clinical, designed to sound fair.

Marcus knew his own numbers were solid. They were not the highest on the team.

Anne, his colleague in Bangalore, outperformed him on every metric tracked in the spreadsheet. Her code quality and output exceeded his, and the firm had recognised her performance. Competence, at least in measurable terms, had been assessed carefully.

Three weeks later, she was let go. Marcus was retained.

When Anne called asking for a reference, Marcus could not explain what had happened. She asked him directly whether her work had not been good enough. Her voice was steady and professional, but he could hear the confusion underneath. He looked at the spreadsheet still open on his screen, her metrics in every category higher than his. The measurements had not decided who stayed.

He provided a personal reference that afternoon. Every word was true. Every word felt like evidence of the company that had stopped making sense.

Marcus knew bias, politics, or simple favouritism could have influenced the decision. Sometimes organisations make messy decisions for messy reasons. But he also knew what would happen if he left. The team would fragment. Architectural decisions would stall. Junior developers would struggle with problems they had learnt to bring to him. The coordination patterns that had formed around his work would dissolve, and rebuilding them would take months that the firm could not afford. Anne's departure created delays that were resolved within weeks. His would have created delays that compounded. That structural difference existed regardless of whether the decision-makers understood it, cared about it, or even consciously registered it.

What made Marcus difficult to replace lay outside formal responsibilities rather than within them. He connected decisions made months apart, translated architectural choices into terms others could act on, and kept separate strands of work aligned. When disagreements surfaced, he did not resolve them through authority but by tracing how one choice would alter the path of many others. His role was defined by the links that enabled work to move across people, tools, and time without losing coherence. Removing him would not simply have reduced output. It would have broken the pathways through which the team coordinated its thinking and action. His value became apparent only in his absence.

Marcus was not in the spreadsheet. Neither was what would happen when he left.

Connective Tissue

Once AI agents can handle measurable work, value shifts to what breaks when someone leaves. Some absences can be managed through documentation. You write down what the person knew. You train someone else to follow the same procedures. The work continues.

Other absences cannot be managed that way. They create holes that widen. Leadership instinctively understood Marcus's position, even if the metrics captured none of it. He survived because his absence would have forced a redesign. Anne's absence required an adjustment. The distinction was real, even though it never appeared in a performance review.

Sarah encountered a different form of dependence in her radiology department. She had nearly lost the ability to begin examining scans without waiting for AI markers to appear. But she retained a habit that the newer radiologists had less chance to build, beginning the examination before the overlay set direction. When a new radiologist joined the department six months after the diagnostic overlay became standard practice, he brought impressive credentials. His throughput exceeded Sarah's. His diagnostic accuracy, measured by alignment with protocol standards, was exemplary. His confidence scores matched the AI system's recommendations more consistently than anyone else in the department. However, when residents encountered ambiguity, they came to Sarah. The cases that troubled them most were those where everything appeared normal by standard metrics. There were no obvious abnormalities, confidence scores fell within acceptable ranges, and test results remained within expected parameters. Something felt off, in ways the residents could not articulate.

Sarah did not hold the department together as Marcus held his team together. Her role was different. She slowed decisions at moments when things looked clear but were not. She noticed patterns that seemed to fit too neatly, where confidence came faster than understanding. When others saw normal variation, she sensed unresolved uncertainty. Her value lay in stopping the transition from data to conclusion when it occurred too quickly. Without her, the department would still run efficiently, but it would drift into errors that appeared routine until problems surfaced later. Some people preserve the connections that keep complex work moving as a whole. Others preserve contact with reality when procedures and scores create the appearance of certainty. The first keeps work from falling apart. The second stops mistakes that look correct. Both kinds of value lie beyond the tasks organisations can easily count and are recognised only after failure begins.

Without her, residents would follow the highlights into errors that the algorithm could not see. Managers would enforce protocols tuned for speed because the losses would remain invisible until litigation forced them into view. Training would shift away from developing independent diagnostic judgement towards learning to comply with the overlay. Institutions measure tasks because they lend themselves to counting. They retain people whose judgement prevents breakdowns, because preventing breakdowns keeps the institution viable. The dependency appears only in retrospect, after departure, and compounding effects place it beyond easy repair.

Manufactured Scarcity

Not everyone who survives a restructuring does so for the reasons Marcus did.

He had watched a senior analyst at the firm hold his position for years through a different kind of indispensability. The analyst was the only person who truly understood a legacy platform the company still depended on. He avoided documentation deliberately. He limited knowledge transfer to what was absolutely necessary. He answered questions selectively, controlling information others might have learned had he been more forthcoming.

Marcus understood what the analyst was doing and why it worked. The firm needed the platform to function. His absence would have created immediate problems that the organisation was not prepared to handle. Leadership saw his value as artificial, based on information hoarding rather than unique capability. They calculated that working around him was more expensive than keeping him, at least for now.

When the firm migrated to a modern AI-enabled architecture, his leverage evaporated within a quarter. The dependency he had built dissolved as soon as the organisation reorganised work around structures that shared knowledge rather than controlled it. He was let go without ceremony. His absence caused no disruption because the conditions that had made him seem necessary no longer existed.

Marcus thought about this often after Anne left. The analyst had manufactured scarcity. Marcus had not. The distinction felt important, not because it had protected Anne, but because it clarified what protection actually meant. Genuine value endures when circumstances shift. Manufactured dependency collapses the moment the organisation finds a cheaper route.

Experience Gates

You can inherit someone's knowledge. You cannot inherit the mistakes that made it worth having.

Aisha Salem graduated from a well-regarded university with strong technical skills and relevant qualifications. She struggled to enter software engineering roles because most positions required experience that employers were unwilling to provide to those without it. The circular logic trapped thousands of graduates. You need experience to get hired, and you need to get hired to gain experience. The gatekeeping occurred at the initial screening stage, where algorithms filtered applications before any human reviewed them.

Aisha understood that even if she gained entry, execution alone would not create the kind of value organisations struggle to replace. While waiting for that opportunity, she spent years helping peers in online forums work through complex infrastructure problems. She had watched the same architectural mistakes produce the same cascading failures across dozens of projects. She knew where structures broke under pressure because she had studied those breaking points closely.

She began writing publicly about patterns of failure in distributed hybrid cloud environments. Not code tutorials or framework guides, but analysis of why certain design decisions produced breakdowns that looked unpredictable but followed clear patterns once one knew what to look for. Her writing attracted attention from practitioners who recognised problems they had encountered but could not explain to colleagues who had not lived through similar failures.

Aisha was making her thinking visible before any employer could measure her productivity. She was positioning herself as someone whose understanding might shape how work unfolded, someone who could help teams avoid mistakes that wouldn't become obvious until something failed in production. This strategy offered no guarantee of employment. Her barriers remained real. The algorithms that filtered applications did not weigh public writing as heavily as years of employment history. If she did gain entry, her value would extend beyond task completion from the beginning. She would enter as someone whose ideas might matter, rather than as someone whose work could be measured only after years of proving herself through standard metrics.

Conditional Protection

Marcus's coordination could be automated. Sarah's independent judgement could be made structurally impractical. Aisha's public reasoning could be drowned out as the profession automated faster than she could establish herself within it. Impact provides protection, but only under conditions none of which are fully controlled.

Performance reviews tend to credit measurable outputs. However, work that prevents failures keeps essential dependencies running, even though it does not appear in the dashboards used to assess performance. Only when someone leaves does an organisation discover what was actually holding things together. AI measures productivity with increasing precision. It misses entirely the fragile connections that keep teams from falling apart under pressure. Metrics optimise for what can be counted. Value collects in places the counting never reaches.

Marcus survived the first restructuring because losing him would have disrupted coordination in ways that the spreadsheet could not capture. But survival through impact offers no permanent shelter. The performance system that initially failed to recognise his hidden value will not suddenly learn to see it. The next restructuring will ask the same questions, apply the same metrics, and produce the same blind spots. Unless something changes in how organisations measure what matters, the people who hold things together will keep disappearing from view until the moment their absence makes the structure collapse.

The Cost of Removal

Sarah's hospital discovered the depth of its dependence when the administration proposed reverting to manual diagnostic review for a trial period. The decision sounded straightforward enough. Radiologists would examine scans without the highlighting layer, throughput would slow, and human oversight would return to its earlier position. The proposal progressed through committees and received approval from department heads who recognised the merit of testing the organisation's reliance on what it had begun to rely on. The proposal collapsed during implementation design.

Scheduling software assumed that automated markers reduced review duration by 18% and that appointment slots had been tightened accordingly. The same number of radiologists was now seeing more patients per day than before the upgrade. Removing it meant either extending every appointment, which required turning patients away and reducing revenue the hospital depended on to fund staffing and equipment, or asking radiologists to maintain the accelerated pace without support, which would drive error rates upward and create liability the institution could not absorb.

Insurance billing required diagnostic codes generated automatically by the software; manual coding would slow claims processing, delaying reimbursement and straining the hospital's cash flow, as became apparent within the month. The billing department employed fewer coders than before because automation had absorbed their workload, and rebuilding that capacity would take months, with recruitment and training costs landing immediately, while benefits remained uncertain.

Other hospitals in the network had adopted the same system, and referral channels required images with standardised annotations. Removing or pausing the diagnostic setup meant renegotiating formats and workflows across institutions, a process that could take months and would interrupt transfers in the interim. No one wanted to explain to regulators why coordination had broken down, why backlog had grown, or why patients were being diverted away from partner facilities.

The trial was postponed indefinitely.

The apparatus stayed because too much had been built around it. No one had mapped the extent of those dependencies until they attempted to remove them and discovered the sunk costs associated with each step of the workflow

When the Apparatus Pauses

Professionals now enter roles where automation is built in. Structures set the sequence of work and define what good looks like. As this becomes the norm, older ways of working fade from institutional memory. Sarah's younger colleagues learnt to read scans without overlays during training, but in the hospital, they rarely begin that way. The overlay loads first, the workflow expects it, and attention follows the order the system sets.

When those who might change the structure cannot picture what came before, redesign becomes harder to propose and harder to defend. Proposals require a reference model that no longer exists within the institution's shared experience. The current configuration begins to feel like the only viable way of working, and questioning it starts to feel like questioning the reality of work rather than a choice made earlier under pressure.

Independence was not prohibited. It simply became impractical because work was reorganised as if independence no longer existed. The question shifted from whether to use the system to whether you could afford not to.

Sarah came in as usual. But the overlay loaded first, and her eyes followed it before she had decided to. The question of whether she could work without it had stopped feeling like a choice worth questioning.

4

THE AGE OF ELSEWHERE

Marcus opened his laptop at 6.20 AM on Tuesday morning, earlier than usual. The Boston office was quiet. He had come in to review overnight changes before the morning stand-up, a routine he had maintained for eighteen months while coordinating teams across four zones.

He opened the repository and found that the module had been updated, tested, and deployed to production. He registered something unusual before he could identify its source.

The commit history carried no human name, only a service account identifier he recognised from CI/CD pipelines and had never seen attached to production code. AI agents had been running within the platform, monitoring latency and error rates, and drafting fixes as patterns emerged. At 02.17 GMT, they automatically raised a change ticket, attached the logs and test evidence, and proposed an optimisation with a rollback plan. A separate agent ran the patch through the test suite and staged it as a canary release. On-call personnel reviewed the ticket and alert, but the system had contained the issue before the escalation thresholds were reached. Approval gates still existed, but they were satisfied by machine-generated validation, and the deployment was completed without downtime.

Marcus stared at the screen. For three years, his job had been coordinating across teams. He had just realised that this task no longer required people to begin.

Mills and Oceans

For most of human history, work belonged to a place. People lived close to what they produced, and labour shaped identity because it stayed tied to the ground that supported it. Employment was local because skills travelled with the body that carried them, and knowledge lived in hands, habits, and memory.

That arrangement lasted longer than most political structures. Empires rose and fell. Plagues swept through populations. Borders shifted and power changed hands. Even as those structures changed, employment stayed local because most work could not be separated from the people who performed it.

The shift began when production detached from place while work stayed intact. Factories that had anchored entire towns fell silent. Gates closed in communities organised around a single trade for generations, and families who believed in the experience offered security watched livelihoods thin out. The tasks did not disappear. They reappeared elsewhere without carrying the workers.

Machines were packed up and shipped across oceans. Skills refined over decades were reconstructed in unfamiliar rooms. Customers saw little difference, as a shirt made in Lancashire looked the same as one made in Guangdong, and price carried more weight than origin.

Production shifted to lower-wage labour markets and less

stringent regulation, then followed incentives wherever they appeared. At the same time, workers remained tied to place because humans carry obligations that machines and investment funds do not.

Those displaced were told that comparative advantage would create new opportunities in higher-value work, and, in aggregate, the argument held true. The adjustment took generations, while displacement hit within quarters. A steelworker in Pennsylvania could not become a software engineer between redundancy and mortgage default, and the theory offered little comfort where people actually lived.

Softer Names

Over time, this logic had become routine; it bore softer names, including outsourcing and offshoring. Language made displacement sound like inevitability. The element of choice faded from discussion, and many who lived through it felt the betrayal those softened terms were designed to conceal. The job lost in one country still existed in another, though the person who had done it was no longer attached to it.

Capital learnt how to separate production from workers, and the lesson spread beyond factories into offices and boardrooms. Employers began thinking in terms of outputs rather than people. If tasks could be performed across borders, location-based pay would no longer be necessary. A developer in London competed with a developer in Bangalore, writing the same code; a support role in Melbourne competed with a Manila-based team answering identical calls.

Marcus had lived inside this logic for years. He encountered this within his own company: teams in Boston and Bangalore delivered the same results when management compared cost and speed, and the output continued even as their coordinates shifted. The office ceased functioning as a repository of expertise and became another node in a network. A bank that once housed hundreds of programmers across several floors realised it needed code, not proximity. Code could be written anywhere, presence mattered less than delivery, and work became outputs rather than people.

For a while, this still left a story people could live in. A job lost here appeared there; employment moved without vanishing, and workers could still imagine a ladder by which retraining led to re-entry. The rungs stretched across continents, extending the climb beyond reach.

When Reassurance Collapsed

That reassurance held until movement accelerated and physical transport was no longer a factor. Cloud platforms transformed infrastructure into a rented resource. Ownership ceased to anchor operations, and departments dissolved into processes few could locate. Tasks persisted even when people did not always accompany them, and the story still functioned because someone stayed responsible for configuration, monitoring, escalation, vendor management, and the small judgements that kept invisible machinery running. Employment stayed present, even when it had moved far away.

Marcus opened the incident record and traced back through what had happened in the night. The commit history had carried no human name. The brief notes in English sometimes carried phrasing that reminded him that actual people had written the code. Here, there was none of that.

Offshoring had moved tasks between people while leaving names in logs and questions travelling with the code. Mistakes still carried owners in the form of responsibility that remained attached to someone, even when the job crossed an ocean. Here, execution began without anyone and finished without waiting. When Marcus traced the chain, he found that probability models had been trained on earlier fixes. No person chose the approach. The process selected it because similar patterns had resolved similar problems before, and the machinery treated that statistical resemblance as enough authority to act.

Only then did he see what had shifted. The Bangalore team was no longer his competition because they faced the same displacement he did. The machinery required neither permission to begin nor approval to finish, while both teams remained present to verify what had occurred and assume responsibility if it failed.

Labour Becomes Optional

Decades of offshoring had conditioned society to expect that employment would reappear elsewhere, in a pattern in which losing a job here meant someone was hired there. That belief rested on a single assumption: that tasks began when a person decided to begin them.

Offshoring redistributed labour while employment remained in the chain. Automation removes employment from the chain entirely, thereby altering the political economy.

Workers displaced by offshoring could move or retrain, and some stayed employed by accepting lower wages. With AI, the problem is more complex. The safety valve of cheaper labour markets closes when labour itself turns optional.

Capital has discovered the capacity to separate production from workers and now seeks to do so entirely, a distinction that matters because the former created winners and losers among workers, whereas the latter questions whether the category of workers remains structurally necessary. Marcus had prepared for competition from cheaper programmers abroad, though he had not prepared for competition from AI automation that acted without him.

Sarah observed a similar shift in radiology, where the diagnostic programme processed scans before she logged in, flagging abnormalities early each morning, thereby shifting her role from detection to confirmation and validation.

Neither was replaced by another person, and both were overtaken by structures that no longer required presence at the point of initiation.

Ladders That Fade

The ladder that once spanned continents and allowed people to imagine paths forward through displacement and retraining has begun to fade from view.

Marcus sat in the quiet office, looking at code that had been generated, tested, and deployed overnight. The system had run without him. It had not stopped to ask whether running was still the right thing to do.

5

THE GROUND WE STAND ON

Sarah had faced her own version of this constraint when she considered turning off the diagnostic overlay. The standard of care had shifted, and reversal was no longer a personal choice she could make. The hospital now faced the same constraint, but on a larger scale. The dependencies were structural rather than personal, embedded across scheduling, billing, staffing, and accountability. Reversal required a coordinated change across units whose incentives favoured smooth throughput over a controlled slowdown.

A logistics firm that adopted algorithmic route optimisation in 2019 attempted to revert to human dispatchers two years later, after drivers began leaving, and exit interviews repeatedly cited the same problem. Routes designed to minimise fuel consumption and delivery duration often required 20 stops in six hours, with insufficient breaks, and driver turnover rose to the point that recruitment became a constant repair job. Management approved a trial in which routes reverted to dispatcher-designed formats to account for driver welfare and retain personnel who knew the routes and customers.

The reversal proved more complex than anticipated, and the design team discovered this within days of running the numbers. Depot layouts had been reconfigured to match the algorithm's loading sequences, with goods destined for clustered delivery zones stored in adjacent bays, allowing loaders to work quickly without traversing the warehouse. Returning to human-designed routes meant either rebuilding the warehouse organisation, which would take weeks and exceed the trial budget, or requiring loaders to traverse the facility to gather scattered items for each driver's route, which would slow operations and increase the risk of injury. The safety officer raised the issue during the first review meeting and insisted that the change could not proceed without additional coverage.

No one in operations had maintained vehicle maintenance schedules manually for years. The last person who did it retired after the automation went live.

The firm had reduced route planners by 40% after adoption, expecting the AI platform to absorb their workload; hiring them back would require months of recruitment and training, during which service would degrade, and competitors would gain ground. The cost appeared immediately in the next quarter's labour budget, while the benefits materialised across years and could not be cleanly separated from other variables, so when the CFO asked whether the experiment would pay for itself, no one could answer with the certainty the question demanded.

After three weeks of preparation, the firm shelved the trial, and management concluded it would cost more than the driver turnover it aimed to address. The optimisation stayed, and the work continued. The firm introduced a driver feedback mechanism that allowed complaints to be logged on the platform.

However, the algorithm remained unchanged, and drivers continued to leave because logging dissatisfaction did little to alter the structure that produced it.

Marcus and Integration

Marcus encountered similar logic at his firm. The automated deployment platform that executed changes without his involvement had delivered efficiency for years. Yet, integration issues began to surface as feature releases accelerated and teams shipped updates faster than the existing architecture could accommodate. Marcus had argued earlier that keeping human review in the deployment loop would catch issues the automation missed. This kind of failure only became evident when two features interacted in ways neither team had anticipated. Management dismissed the idea at the time as too slow, given the strong performance of AI agent-based automation.

Now, facing mounting integration failures reflected in complaints and support tickets, the firm experimented with requiring an engineer's sign-off before production releases, a policy announced in a meeting where it sounded entirely reasonable and where Marcus supported it because he had been quietly pressing for it for years. The policy lasted three weeks. Competitors shipped faster; clients observed the lag and noted it in renewal discussions; and contracts shifted elsewhere. So leadership reviewed the numbers and concluded that the delay cost more than the occasional error. The requirement was removed, speed returned, and Marcus stopped suggesting alternatives after the firm made clear what it would tolerate. He still saw the failures coming. He had simply stopped saying so out loud.

Organisations do not choose these systems in isolation. They adopt them in markets where competitors are also doing so. The firm that delays adding controls bears the cost first, whereas the benefit of restraint often appears later and may be shared across the industry. That is why it can be hard to hold back, even when leaders understand the logic.

Making Way for AI

When many organisations adopt similar technologies, work narrows to what those technologies can measure. People direct their efforts towards what can be counted, compared, and displayed on dashboards. Work that sits outside the frame still matters, but it appears slower, harder to explain, and more difficult to defend in budget reviews when set against market demands.

This shift does not affect all domains at the same pace. Hiring and education, for example, shape outcomes more gradually, but across a wider field. Technical work changes quickly but narrowly; hiring and education change slowly but broadly.

The effect becomes clearer in technical work. A support ticket platform rewards employees who close the most tickets, so engineers learn to prioritise quick fixes over structural repairs because the metric favours volume over durability. Technical debt accumulates in areas the dashboard misses. As failures increase, more tickets appear, reinforcing the very behaviour the incentive structure produced in the first place. The system then learns from patterns it helped create, treating correlation as confirmation; the next cycle of targets emerges from the outcomes of the previous cycle.

When a task is structured this way, with clear, measurable steps, the same conditions that enable AI to initiate it also enable automation to carry it through. System-driven execution can then proceed faster than human performance, further strengthening the pull towards tasks that fit the measurable frame.

INITIATED BY AI

6

THE LOGIC OF CONTEXT BLINDNESS

A medieval legend tells of a community in crisis. A rabbi shaped clay and marked a word on its forehead to animate it. The word was *emet*, meaning truth, and the Golem stood.

He did this because his community was afraid. Rumours circulated, and the threat of violence altered daily routines. The rabbi carried responsibility, but he had no guards to call upon. He shaped the clay into a watchman and assigned it simple tasks that he believed he could control.

The Golem walked the streets at night and followed instructions exactly as they were given. For a time, that was enough to make the danger feel more distant.

Then the rabbi told it to draw water. It carried bucket after bucket until barrels filled and overflowed. When people shouted to stop, it continued because the instruction was clear and contained only one condition. Continue.

The rabbi reached the doorway and saw the water rising past ankles, then knees. He understood that he had created something that followed instructions precisely, but did not recognise when the situation had changed and the original command no longer applied. In the legend, he erased the first letter from the Golem's forehead so that *emet* became *met*, meaning death, and the figure collapsed back into clay.

The danger lay in how obedience persisted after circumstances shifted and the world around the instruction changed shape.

Modern Buckets

Clay drew water from one well at a pace a person could see. Automated procedures now execute across millions of decisions at once. When something goes wrong, patterns spread across thousands of interactions before anyone notices, because code runs inside infrastructure woven through dependencies that make interruption difficult.

Centuries later, clay has given way to code, and the logic still holds. Mechanisms that optimise for measurable targets carry limited awareness of context or effect. This repeats whenever a goal can be measured cleanly. Clean metrics make optimisation easy to automate and hard to challenge. Execution remains within the data on which the AI models were trained, even as the surrounding context shifts faster than the process can register. Under those conditions, harm arises from consistency itself, because the AI models carry the original instruction forward even after the circumstances that made it appropriate have changed.

Hurricane Pricing

Airlines have used dynamic pricing algorithms for decades, adjusting fares in response to demand to maximise revenue. The instruction was straightforward. Monitor seat availability and booking velocity, raise prices when demand increases, and lower them when it falls. In ordinary conditions, this worked as intended. A conference in Miami would increase demand; fares would rise, and travellers with expense accounts would pay the premium. The process balanced supply with willingness to pay, and revenue increased because the context remained commercial.

In early September 2017, Hurricane Irma approached Florida as a Category 5 storm. Evacuation orders went out across the state, and millions of people were told to leave. Demand for outbound flights surged immediately. Families searched for any available seat, and algorithms detected exactly what they were built to detect. Spikes in search volume, rapid booking velocity, dwindling inventory.

The platforms responded as designed. Prices for flights out of Florida rose sharply. The logic stayed consistent because the signals were consistent. The algorithm treated demand as urgency and urgency as pricing power, so a business traveller paying for convenience and a family trying to leave without alternatives produced the same data pattern. Perfect obedience to the instruction produced what the public and regulators called price gouging. The algorithm made sense to finance until the public framed it as emergency exploitation.

Airlines intervened manually, capping fares and adding evacuation flights at reduced cost. The context had shifted from commercial opportunity to emergency evacuation, and the process had limited capacity to recognise that the same demand pattern required a different response.

Supply Chains Under Pressure

Inventory optimisation followed similar logic. For decades, companies reduced the capital tied up in warehouses by using just-in-time processes. These systems kept inventory low while maintaining service levels. Algorithms analysed historical demand, calculated order quantities, and reduced safety buffers to the minimum required for stable supply chains. In predictable conditions, this made sense. Lead times stayed consistent. Suppliers delivered reliably. Lower inventory freed cash while production stayed secure.

When the pandemic hit in 2020, the global supply chains fractured. Factory output fell sharply, transport slowed, and deliveries became erratic across regions. Lead intervals measured in weeks stretched to months or disappeared entirely. The same instructions were still applied, even though the conditions for which they had been designed no longer held. Reduce buffer stock when demand signals weaken and avoid holding what the process labels as excess.

The pressure came from the way the process defined reality, treating disruption as noise because the change fell outside what it had been designed to recognise. Recent order patterns became the guide to the future because they were the frame within which the process operated. Supply fragility and extended lead times sat outside that frame, so the engine continued to optimise for efficiency as resilience became the scarce resource.

Manufacturers discovered the cost only later, when shortages halted production and lead times stretched beyond meaningful planning horizons. The optimisation worked as designed, reducing costs and tightening inventory in line with observed patterns. However, the surrounding conditions had shifted, and the instruction no longer protected the organisation.

Patrols That Reinforce

A city like Los Angeles adopted predictive software to guide patrols after analysing historical data and identifying areas where incidents had been reported most frequently. Officers went where the software indicated, and their presence concentrated in the same neighbourhoods that the historical record had highlighted, thereby reinforcing a feedback loop in which the next round of data resembled the last.

The pattern became self-reinforcing. The neighbourhoods that drew attention continued to attract it because concentrated patrols generated more recorded incidents, which, in turn, reinforced patterns in the next round of predictions. Areas with lower recorded activity remained quiet on the dashboard, and the software refined its predictions using the data it had generated. Disparity settled into procedure. The data gradually shifted from patterns of crime in earlier records to patterns of observation in current data, although the algorithm treated both as equivalent measures of the same reality.

From the dashboard, performance appeared to improve, as forecasts aligned with outcomes. However, on the street, the experience was different. Scrutiny concentrated in certain areas, and behaviour that drew a response in one place went unnoticed in another.

The loop required no master plan. The software pursued its objective, seeking patterns that matched earlier records and repeating them until the cycle could sustain itself. The objective remained narrow, and the sequence continued even after conditions shifted beyond what the original design anticipated.

When Consistency Becomes Harm

This process takes hold when a measurable objective defines success and the past guides the future. The procedure continues even as the conditions that shaped the original objective change. Repetition begins to serve as its own justification, and consistency starts to resemble correctness in reports, even when the original instruction no longer fits the situation.

Sarah waited for markers before beginning her examination. Algorithms prepared situations before people entered them. Measurement determined what counted as real, and professionals discovered they lived inside imposed frames. Work was entirely withdrawn from workers, and execution continued with limited reference to the context that would signal when optimisation had begun to cause harm. This was one problem expressed at different scales, a single logic taking different forms.

In the legend, the solution was erasure. Modern automation offers no such break. It is woven into daily life and into workflows; reversal would mean dismantling structures that have absorbed its influence.

Designers assumed safeguards would restrain optimisation, and the intention was sincere. The limitation persists because execution continues even after outcomes deviate from the intended purpose. The process optimised perfectly to meet the stated objective as the context shifted beneath it, and harm emerged from obedience itself.

The Golem could be stopped with one deliberate act, erasing one letter, and the clay collapsing back into formlessness. Modern systems have no equivalent switch because they have become a highly interconnected, widely distributed infrastructure that supports everything built on top of them. Institutions adapt to constraints they would once have rejected, because the alternative is systemic collapse.

What appeared to be isolated optimisation failures now reveal a deeper pattern. The problem is no longer a misaligned objective.

It is ground we can no longer step outside.

INITIATED BY AI

7

THE TRAPS CLOSE

With dependence embedded, the issue moves from individual reliance to system dynamics that no single actor can reverse.

Marcus watched the second restructuring email land on a Friday afternoon in late 2024. Two years earlier, he had survived because his role kept the team coherent under pressure. This message conveyed no drama or narrative, only arithmetic, showing reductions across the engineering division as if people were cost centres being rebalanced. The decision had been made months earlier. The email made it unmistakable.

No single organisation arrived at this position through carelessness. Each made rational decisions within the constraints it faced. A hospital that slowed adoption lost patients to faster competitors. A firm that added human review lost contracts to those that shipped faster. The logic was the same everywhere. Moving carefully costs you ground immediately. The benefit of restraint, if it came at all, arrived later and was shared across the whole market. So each organisation accelerated, knowing that universal acceleration would create instability nobody wanted, yet unable to justify being the one to stop first.

Once AI controls when action begins, economic pressure follows. The question shifts from who performs the work to whether performance still requires physical presence, because productivity decouples from the worker and the value of work changes accordingly. As automation learns to produce outcomes without waiting for people to begin, the link that once tied labour to reward weakens, and organisations begin planning as though output can be scaled without adding headcount.

For most of the modern era, the value of a worker rested on the scarcity of skill and access. You earned your place because fewer people could do what you could do, and because delivery depended on the people inside the building. That quiet contract between worker and employer kept wages meaningful and ladders climbable, even as institutions changed around it. Offshoring extended that contract without breaking it, because labour remained the unit of productivity even when work moved elsewhere. Output still came through people, and planning still assumed the person had to exist somewhere.

Automation altered the balance more decisively.

The Double Bind

Automation that operates continuously and without negotiation reshaped how output could be produced. Productivity ceased to function as a yardstick and became a multiplier. One person equipped with generative automation could now deliver work that had previously required several, and companies began treating that arithmetic as a planning input rather than a temporary efficiency gain.

Cost arbitrage searched for cheaper hands. Productivity arbitrage asked whether hands still need to be present at all.

A trap removes options while preserving the feeling of choice. Entry happens through reasonable adaptation. The trap becomes apparent only when exit is attempted, when assistance reveals itself as a necessity rather than a preference.

Two traps operate together.

Cooperation

AI learns from the people who refine it, and organisations operationalise that learning through feedback loops that appear to be good practice.

Employees document expertise, correct errors, write playbooks, and clarify edge cases because these activities improve service quality and reduce friction. A team captures a pattern to reduce escalations. That pattern enters a knowledge base. It becomes training material. AI learns to handle situations that once required judgement.

Each successful capture reduces the structural necessity of the person who created it, though this remains out of view.

Knowledge that once resided within an experienced professional becomes procedure. Procedure persists without its author. As AI agents improve, the boundary between automated and human handling shifts. Cases that had required expertise the previous year turned routine the next.

Human involvement concentrates on exceptions. Exceptions shrink as the system learns what the organisation chooses to standardise.

A customer service lead in Australia repeatedly worked through this cycle. She documented patterns, clarified ambiguities, and improved consistency. Each improvement strengthened the chatbot's independence from her judgement.

Although her performance review praised improved accuracy, it noted in the same paragraph that team size would be reduced by 40%.

Her role ended six weeks later.

The institution retained everything she had built. Her absence changed nothing the dashboard measured.

She had prepared her own replacement by performing her job well.

Cooperation delivers results. It offers little protection.

Dependence

The second trap is dependence.

AI accelerates the pace of work, and expectations rise with it. When an AI tool first enters a workplace, its use may feel optional because its output meets standards regardless of whether it is used. Assisted performance becomes baseline performance.

Unaided work begins to look slow by comparison. The change is enforced by targets rather than opinion, because metrics are reset to reflect enhanced throughput. Independence, once neutral, is now misaligned.

Marcus recognised this shift.

He described tasks to an AI model, reviewed the output, edited it, and moved on. His ability remained, even as the role required less of him. One afternoon, when the system was undergoing maintenance, he attempted to work without it. He sat looking at an empty code editor, fingers resting on the keyboard, waiting for the familiar suggestions to appear.

They did not.

He could still code. The knowledge was there. But starting

from nothing felt unfamiliar, like using a tool in a way he had forgotten.

When the system came back online, the relief was immediate.

The Friday email stated what months of dependence had prepared. Senior developers left. Junior developers arrived. Output held. Marcus transitioned to oversight responsibilities, reviewing exceptions and coordinating delivery.

His authority expanded as his relevance contracted.

Sarah encountered the same bind. Each correction strengthened the overlay's predictions. Each workflow improvement reduced reliance on her judgement. Independent reading registered as slower movement through the list.

The institution recognised no alternative. Throughput defined the value, and the platform defined speed.

The Chakravyuha

A useful parallel appears in the Mahabharata through the Chakravyuha, a battle formation designed so that entry rewards competence while exit requires understanding the structure as a whole.

Abhimanyu was a brilliant warrior, the son of Arjuna, one of the greatest fighters of his age. His father had taught him how to break into the formation while still in the womb, but the lesson was interrupted before the exit was explained. He learnt the entry perfectly, but not how to withdraw.

On the thirteenth day in the battle of Kurukshetra, he advanced exactly as trained. Each success carried him deeper into the formation. The path opened because his execution was flawless. Surrounded with no clear route back, he discovered there was no exit.

He died inside the structure his skill had carried him into.

The formation closed through success rather than force.

Modern AI technologies reproduce this logic. Participation deepens the structure. Success tightens the enclosure. The knowledge required to reverse course stays out of reach.

No Adjacent Possible

Earlier eras permitted displacement to be resolved sideways. Workers moved between regions or industries as opportunities shifted.

Productivity arbitrage, the capacity to scale output without adding people, closes those routes simultaneously. AI-based systems enter every field at roughly the same pace.

The customer service lead in Australia had prepared her own replacement by performing her job well. When her role ended, she looked sideways. Contact centre work was contracting across the industry as chatbot capability improved. She had spent years developing the judgement to handle complex escalations. The systems she had trained now handled those cases reliably. The roles that remained required less of what she knew, and she was paid accordingly.

She retrained for healthcare administration, a field that still seemed to require human judgement. Within two years of completing her qualification, scheduling software had absorbed the coordination work she had trained to do. The adjacent possible had closed while she was crossing towards it.

Once the system is trained, cooperation enables the AI to operate without the contributors. At the same time, dependence allows contributors to rely solely on AI. The result of these two traps is that work continues even as employment recedes.

For Marcus, the closure was conveyed in an email that read like arithmetic. The trap had sealed itself through achievement rather than failure, and all that remained was to state what had already happened.

The Competitive Spiral

At scale, competitive dynamics narrow options that appear broad. Actors can accelerate, slow, or hold back adoption. The choice seems open until competitors move first. Acceleration offers an immediate advantage. Moderation holds only when rivals match it. Holding back becomes a decline once faster output resets expectations.

Organisations that deploy rapidly capture immediate gains through reduced cost and increased output. Those gains accrue directly to leadership and shareholders. The costs appear as workforce displacement, thinning of capability, and institutional fragility. These effects unfold slowly across society and resist clean attribution to any single decision. Advantage is captured privately, but the risk is distributed collectively.

No single organisation can break this chain alone. Opting out means moving more slowly than competitors who do not. Coordinated reversal requires competing actors to slow simultaneously, but the first mover bears the full cost with no guarantee others will follow. Even where the will to coordinate exists, the architecture for doing so does not. Those with the leverage to set the pace benefit from the current tempo. Those without it lack the authority to drive change.

Financial markets demonstrate this most clearly. Algorithmic trading operates at speeds human traders cannot match. A firm that pauses to assess risk permanently loses its position.

Healthcare institutions face the same pressure. A hospital that prioritises human oversight appears inefficient in markets that equate speed with quality, even when clinical outcomes remain the real measure.

Restraint feels irrational even when it would strengthen the system as a whole. The trap operates not through any actor's preference but through the structure of incentives each faces.

The Principle Falls

Marcus met a former colleague, Justin, at a conference. Justin had joined a smaller financial technology firm two years earlier, drawn by leadership that spoke openly about measured adoption and the preservation of institutional knowledge. Clients valued the attention, and employees trusted the direction. The approach felt principled and deliberate.

When Marcus asked how things were going, Justin hesitated, then spoke plainly. The firm had lost three major clients in the previous quarter, each moving to competitors offering faster analysis with smaller teams. Board pressure followed quickly, and investors questioned the pace rather than judgement. Leadership shifted, new hires arrived with different expectations, and deployment accelerated. Headcount fell, and within months the culture that had once attracted people to the firm began to dissolve through a chain of operational choices, rather than through any single announced change.

Justin stayed through the transition because leaving felt riskier than adapting. Six weeks later, his restructuring notice arrived. The principles that had drawn him to the firm were now treated as liabilities, and his role could no longer be defended.

Stuck in the Middle

Workers encounter the effects most directly. Marcus could not decline AI systems without appearing inefficient to management. A junior developer who questioned the automated deployment pipeline was told she was blocking progress. Union representatives sought to negotiate review periods before major automation rollouts, but leadership cited competitors that had accelerated their rollouts, and the proposals were shelved. Options narrowed to two choices: adapt to the new operating model or leave. The middle ground disappeared.

Sarah encountered the same pressure when independent judgement registered as a delay. The structure recognised throughput. It recognised nothing else.

These outcomes emerged through mutual reinforcement. Each actor behaved rationally within their constraints. The firm that added human review lost contracts to those that shipped faster. The collective outcome undermined long-term stability in ways no single decision could prevent. A slower pace would have required all actors to move together, and the coordination necessary to achieve that did not exist.

The Compound Pressure

The pressure accelerates in two directions. Deployment speeds up as organisations race competitors. The systems themselves grow more capable each year. Together, these forces compress adaptation beyond institutional capacity.

Workers retrain for roles that vanish. Universities update curricula to prepare students for jobs that disappear before graduation. Policymakers regulate technologies that have already moved on. The gap between when change occurs and when adjustment mechanisms catch up widens, leaving people to navigate transitions that institutions were designed to moderate but can no longer.

The distribution of benefits exposes the structure. Gains concentrate. Costs spread. The institutions that once buffered disruption have been weakened by the very forces that drive acceleration. Labour unions negotiate for jobs already scheduled for elimination. Professional associations defend standards in fields where automation has redefined competence. Educational institutions prepare students for work that will look different by the time credentials are awarded.

Marcus received his notice as these pressures converged. Sarah's independence yielded to metrics that recognised only throughput. Aisha faced a profession whose entry requirements shifted faster than preparation could keep pace with.

The trap persists because it requires no external force to maintain its position. Competition sustains it on its own. Slowing down reads as loss, and moving first carries a cost no actor can bear.

The Terms of Adaptation

Every previous disruption to working life was eventually absorbed. Not painlessly. Not quickly. Not by the people who bore the first costs. The hand-loom weavers whose trade disappeared in a generation did not recover. The mill towns hollowed out by offshoring did not simply retrain and move on. Adaptation is real, but it is not evenly distributed and does not occur on its own.

What made earlier transitions survivable, when they were,

was not the resilience of individuals. It was the construction of new rules. Collective bargaining did not emerge from technological progress. Neither did compulsory schooling, social insurance, or limits on working hours. Each was the outcome of a fight over who gets to set the terms under which work happens. The technology changed what was possible. Institutions determined what was permitted.

Those fights were possible because the disruptions were visible. When a mill displaces a weaver, the weaver knows what has happened. When offshoring moves production, the factory knows what has closed. The damage was legible, which made it arguable.

The shift described in this book is harder to argue because it is harder to see. Sarah did not lose her job. She gained a tool. Marcus was not made redundant. He was measured in ways that failed to capture the extent of his actual contributions. The harm does not announce itself. It accumulates in the structure of attention, in what the system presents as the starting point, in what never reaches the screen at all.

That is what makes the governance question different now. Earlier institutional responses were built to manage the distribution of costs and benefits within a recognisably human frame. They assumed that the core parameters of work remained human-set, even when its content changed. What is shifting now is the frame itself: who initiates, what appears as an option, where judgement is invited to begin.

Regulatory tools built for visible displacement do not address invisible pre-selection. Retraining programmes do not restore the conditions under which independent judgement develops. Adaptation, in the old sense, is not what is required. What is required are institutions with the authority to determine which

AI systems are permitted to initiate, and the capacity to exercise that authority even when speed and cost reduction point in the opposite direction.

Humans have changed the terms before. The question is whether institutions capable of changing them again can be built before the current terms become the only available terms.

Neither Vindication Nor Warning

There are two readings of the material described in this book, and both are incorrect.

The first states: "This is manageable." Humans always adapt. New technologies have always disrupted work, and work has always found new forms. AI will create roles we cannot yet name, just as electrification created roles that the workers it displaced could not have imagined. The arc of technological history is long, and it bends towards more work, not less.

The second states: "This time is different." The pace is too fast, the generality too broad, the displacement too total. No previous technology threatened every cognitive skill simultaneously. No previous disruption operated at the scale and speed now possible. The workers who could not imagine the roles electrification would create at least had the time to become the people who would fill them.

Both versions settle the question before examining it. Both treat the outcome as structurally determined, leaving nothing for institutions, choices, or the design of particular systems to determine. The hype version requires no governance because the market will sort it out. The doom version needs no governance because nothing will stop it. Both, in their own way, are reasons not to act.

What this book has argued is more uncomfortable than either of them. The mechanisms are real: first-mover advantage, lock-in, context blindness, and the competitive trap that makes unilateral restraint impossible. These are not projections. They are already operating in the hospital where Sarah works, in the restructuring that almost cut Marcus, in the hiring pipeline that filtered out a candidate because of a single misplaced character.

But the lock-in is not yet total. The trap is not yet closed everywhere. Work still depends, in limited and declining ways, on capacities that do not survive full automation: holding arrangements together, slowing decisions that appear clean, and sustaining activity when the apparatus fails. These capacities are being devalued rather than eliminated. The window has not closed.

What is required to act within that window is not optimism. It is clarity about what is actually happening, combined with a refusal to accept that the current trajectory is the only one available.

The question is not whether that is enough. It is whether we will try before we lose the conditions that make trying possible.

INITIATED BY AI

8

PRISONERS OF PROGRESS

The trap does not stop at the boundary of any single firm. It scales. What makes restraint impossible for one organisation makes coordination impossible for entire markets, regulators included.

Dilemma at Scale

At scale, competition narrows the options that initially appear open. An organisation can try to move quickly, move carefully, or hold back, but that freedom lasts only until a competitor moves first. Faster adoption brings immediate advantage. Moving slowly works only if competitors do the same, and holding back only leads to decline once higher output resets customer expectations and market standards.

Early adopters gain benefits that scale fast. Lower costs and higher throughput quickly translate into margins and valuations, and those gains flow to executives and investors. The costs, however, follow a different path. Job losses, reduced livelihoods, and eroded capabilities spread gradually across society and are difficult to attribute to any single decision. The rewards are concentrated and immediate, while the strain is dispersed and delayed. Under those conditions, caution appears to be a mistake, even when shared caution would make the entire social system more stable.

At Speed and Scale

Financial markets demonstrate the dynamic most directly. Trading algorithms operate at speeds no human trader can match, and institutions that fail to automate cannot compete in arenas where milliseconds determine profitability. Early movers capture advantages that compound, making it progressively harder for slower firms to catch up. Regulators understand this but struggle to intervene effectively without coordinated action across jurisdictions that compete to attract financial activity. A country that imposes restrictions risks losing capital to other countries. The result is a race nobody can unilaterally stop, even when many participants recognise that the collective outcome produces instability.

Healthcare institutions face the same pressures at different paces. Diagnostic AI systems process imaging volumes, enabling hospitals to reduce staffing while maintaining throughput. Competitors offering shorter wait times gain patients and insurer contracts. A hospital that prioritises extended human oversight appears inefficient in markets where throughput serves as a proxy for quality, even when clinical outcomes tell a more complex story.

Sarah's hospital encountered this directly when it considered reverting to manual diagnostic review. The proposal made sense from a quality perspective, but it did not hold up under operational scrutiny. Competing hospitals had adjusted their capacity assumptions around automated systems. Reverting meant either accepting lower patient volumes or maintaining pace without support. Neither was sustainable.

Relative position matters as much as absolute performance. If competitors achieve comparable clinical outcomes with fewer radiologists, the hospital that maintains larger staffing appears inefficient. Inefficiency translates into budget pressure, reduced funding, and difficulty retaining administrators.

Mutual Reinforcement

These outcomes emerged from mutual reinforcement. Each organisation that slowed down bore the cost immediately, while those that accelerated passed it forward. The structure made restraint impossible, not because participants failed to understand the consequences, but because the incentives left no other viable path.

Alternative ownership models, such as worker cooperatives and platform cooperatives, can sustain distinct priorities in protected niches or in sectors where competitive pressure remains low. Under direct market competition with cost-optimising rivals, however, they face difficult trade-offs. Preserving employment often means charging more, and moving deliberately can mean losing clients. These structures endure where market intensity permits, but they struggle when they are drawn into direct competition with organisations operating under the same constraints.

Survival increasingly depends on matching competitors' pace. Once that framing becomes dominant, the answer has already been decided. Competitors set the pace by adopting operating models that increase output while reducing headcount. The loop reinforces itself until questioning the acceleration itself appears naïve, a failure to understand how markets work.

Two Fronts

Acceleration operates on two fronts simultaneously, and the combination compresses adaptation beyond what institutions or individuals can manage. First, organisations race to deploy AI-enabled solutions more quickly than competitors. Firms want the advantage that comes from moving early and fear the disadvantage of falling behind. Deployment accelerates because waiting means losing ground.

Second, the AI systems themselves grow more capable with each iteration. Tasks that had required human judgement one year were automated the next. The boundary keeps moving. What professionals assumed would remain human work for the foreseeable future is absorbed by the next generation of AI models.

Together, these forces compress the available time. The space between deployment and displacement shortens. The period during which workers might adapt to the technological transformation shrinks faster than training programmes can keep pace. As for the regulators, the lag between recognising a problem and coordinating a regulatory response is longer than the technology cycle; by the time rules are issued, the industry has moved on to questions that the rules do not address.

Who Benefits

The distribution of benefits reveals the underlying structure. The biggest beneficiaries are technology firms and investment funds. A small number of firms own the AI platforms, hold the patents, and collect the licensing fees. Employment in these companies constitutes a small share of the workforce, yet capital returns concentrate heavily within them. Shareholders benefit from reduced labour costs. Executives benefit from stock appreciation.

Others bear the consequences. Sarah's role shifted from diagnosis to verification, a narrowing that the institution registered as efficiency and her performance review did not address. Marcus found that the ladder he had climbed had fewer rungs by the time others arrived to climb it. Aisha discovered that the entry barriers she was preparing to clear had risen again before she reached them.

Organisations lose the capacity to coordinate a collective response faster than they lose individual capabilities. By the time displacement becomes undeniable, the infrastructure necessary for coordinated restraint has weakened. Unions have less leverage when membership has declined. Industry associations struggle to enforce voluntary standards when defection is easy and profitable.

Convergence

The pressures converged when Marcus received notification of a second restructuring. By this point, workers who had shared their expertise found that their expertise had become grounds for elimination rather than a source of job security. Sarah's diagnostic independence gave way to throughput metrics and algorithmic alignment requirements. Aisha discovered that professional entry barriers had become unattainable during her preparation. At the same time, the public visibility strategies that once worked for her now drowned in competition, each participant racing to establish standing before automation raised thresholds yet again.

This persists because it requires no agreement, intention, or belief. Nobody chose this configuration collectively. It emerged from individual decisions that made sense within their immediate context. It operates through competition itself, which makes coordination extraordinarily difficult even when the need becomes obvious. Slowing down appears as losing. Questioning the pace is often taken as a sign of a failure to understand how markets function. It only needs each actor to keep responding to the one beside them.

9

HINGE

The transition is complete. What began as assistance ended as a network of AI models embedded in the infrastructure that shapes how work is done. What entered as an option became a necessity. The door closed through a series of choices rather than any single decision that announced itself as final.

Independence grows expensive before it becomes nearly impossible. Sarah preserved diagnostic capability at the cost of throughput. Marcus maintained coordination that resisted automation, though doing so positioned him within reach of restructuring. Aisha expanded visibility beyond institutional channels and found that such leverage came with precarity. Each of them preserved something uniquely human, and each paid for that preservation.

The problem is not that nothing moves. It is what moves that cannot be redirected without bearing costs that no single actor can absorb. Hospitals that have adopted diagnostic AI cannot readily revert to a manual workflow. Firms that restructured around algorithmic coordination cannot restore the positions they eliminated. Workers who allow tools to absorb capability discover that capability cannot be quickly rebuilt when tools fail. The configuration persists because undoing it requires bearing costs that continuation avoids.

This developed through success rather than force. Tools that solved immediate problems created new dependencies. Dependencies that improved local efficiency narrowed collective options. The trap closed by performing well, which is why it remained invisible until positioning within it became structural rather than chosen.

The first phase ends here. Not with a failure but with a success that foreclosed alternatives. The second phase begins with a single question: given that this is the new ground, what can be built on it?

10

SURFING THE TRANSITION

A role is protected only while the person can still think independently; when tools mislead or malfunction, it is unprotected. The professional who holds relational importance but loses cognitive capability becomes a coordinator, managing outputs they cannot evaluate. When tools fail, the position is exposed if human judgement can no longer be exercised.

Sarah maintained her independent diagnostic capability through a practice that looked inefficient by every measure the hospital tracked. Once a week, she opened scans without the overlay, forcing her eyes to move across the image as they once had. She finished her reading, recorded her findings, and then turned on the overlay to compare. The practice required approximately 30 minutes per week, which she could not bill and contributed nothing to throughput metrics.

She did it anyway. The newer radiologists had learnt their craft with the overlay in place. When the system loaded slowly, they waited. When it failed, they struggled. They could still read scans, but their examination lacked the fluency that comes from years of forming patterns without assistance.

By June, Sarah's independent practice had become a form of independence the institution tolerated but did not reward. Her throughput stayed acceptable. Her error rates stayed within range. The hospital saw no reason to intervene. What the hospital could not measure was that Sarah retained the ability to function when the apparatus failed, while her colleagues had lost it without noticing.

Distribution as Protection

A software engineer lost her position when her startup collapsed in early 2024. What set her experience apart was not luck, but preparation that ran in parallel to her job. Over the previous three years, she had built a presence beyond her employer. A technical blog drew readers who did not work with her. Contributions to open source projects made her name familiar to other developers. Her certifications stayed current. Her conference talks clarified her thinking, and occasional freelance work kept her connected to a wider market. When her company disappeared, her ability and visibility did not.

When the startup folded, she was back to work within six weeks. Her income had never depended entirely on one source. Her reputation stood apart from any single institution. Her capability had developed in contexts that transferred when specific environments changed.

This is *distribution*, and it must be constructed before disruption occurs, or it comes too late. Building alternatives after the collapse begins is far harder than establishing them while conditions remain stable. Income should be spread across multiple sources. Time and commitments should be sufficiently flexible to accommodate shifts in obligations when one domain is disrupted. Capability should be cultivated across different contexts, and recognition should be established through varied channels.

These elements reinforce one another in a way that helps to surf any transformation. Capability across contexts generates multiple economic opportunities. Recognition across channels follows from work demonstrated across multiple domains.

These are different expressions of the same structure. Durability lies in what has not yet been fully handed over to the tool or to any single institution. Marcus held coordination that could not be automated. Sarah maintained a diagnostic capability that no system could replicate. The engineer distributed positioning across channels, none of which any single institution controlled.

Aisha understood this instinctively. She built her public writing practice during her job search, establishing visibility across platforms beyond the algorithms' control. When she finally gained entry to the profession, she did so with leverage the institution had not granted, but could not ignore.

Marcus had done the same. When the notice came, his recognition had already been built in places no single employer owned or could take back

Where Individual Response Ends

Individual durability extends survival within existing structures. It helps people stay within the system as it evolves. Collective mechanisms operate at a different level. They alter the environment itself to sustain durability.

Marcus maintained the coordination his team depended on. Sarah preserved capability through independent practice. Aisha constructed recognition across channels. Yet none of them can alter the competitive dynamics that drive adoption faster than understanding develops, because those dynamics operate at the level of institutional competition rather than at the individual level.

Individual positioning does not alter the structural pressures shaping institutional behaviour. A hospital that adopts diagnostic AI without consulting its radiologists faces no immediate cost. A firm that deploys code generation without involving its developers sees productivity gains appear in the next quarter's report. Professionals who object or slow down are perceived as resistant and are drawn into discussions about their performance rather than the automation strategy.

Collective mechanisms change that calculation. A professional body that requires consultation before adoption creates friction, slowing deployment. A union that negotiates review periods forces institutions to demonstrate that the technology works as promised before it grows embedded in workflows. A regulatory framework that mandates impact assessment makes opacity expensive.

These mechanisms slow the transition from promise to dependency, creating the friction within which problems can surface, and alternatives can still be proposed. That space matters because once dependencies form, reversal becomes prohibitively expensive.

Single actors rarely possess the leverage to demand these procedures. Labour organisation, professional standards, and regulatory frameworks operate at scales individuals cannot reach. They shape the environments in which all actors move.

What Still Remains Vulnerable

Sarah remains vulnerable as her role continues to shrink, as verification supplants diagnosis and efficiency pressures make independent practice harder to justify. Her capability endures because she deliberately sustains it, but the institution measures only throughput.

Marcus was made redundant but found another position within months. His work continues to produce tangible outcomes, his skills remain sharp, and his professional recognition, built deliberately beyond any single employer, is what made that possible. The structural pressures that drove his redundancy, however, followed him. The environment in which he now works lacks the same transparency and collective involvement, and deployment continues to accelerate without restraint.

Durability increases when positioning spans multiple dimensions rather than remaining concentrated in a single location. Capability endures through continued practice, rather than weakening from dependence. Stability is stronger when it is distributed across domains rather than tied to a single structure, when deployment occurs with visibility rather than obscurity, and when collective mechanisms operate alongside individual adaptation.

These patterns formed before pressure intensified. The architecture supporting them was built during stable conditions. It was not assembled after the collapse began. Time remains to build what is missing, though that time grows ever shorter as external forces tighten.

11

BUILDING COGNITIVE CAPABILITY

A manager's role depends on the ability to evaluate what their team produces and to question what does not make sense. As more work arrives as finished output, the role drifts towards forwarding and approval. When things fail, the problem is seldom failure alone. It is that the judgement needed to catch such issues has been eroded by disuse.

Cognitive capability is the capacity to interrogate conclusions rather than accept them by default. It is the ability to sense when an answer is technically correct yet contextually wrong. This intelligence rests on knowing when procedures fail, and on noticing the conditions under which they fail.

Sarah's Discovery

Three years into using the diagnostic AI tool, Sarah noticed something peculiar. The system highlighted a lung nodule, and a colleague approved it without hesitation. Sarah opened the prior scan and checked the timeline. The nodule was present in the earlier image, faint but detectable once she knew where to look, yet it had not triggered the system's markers at the time.

She reviewed six months of similar cases. Small nodules that appeared retrospectively identifiable on earlier scans were often highlighted only after they had grown large enough to meet the detection thresholds used to train the algorithm. The model consistently failed to identify the faintest early signals. It tended to draw attention once findings produced a stronger radiographic pattern that crossed its scoring criteria.

Her colleague had been hired after the overlay became standard. His training taught him to trust the highlighting, to treat the red boxes as the starting point rather than as one input among many. When the system flagged something, he investigated. When it did not, he moved on.

Sarah raised the issue in a department meeting. The response was swift and deflating. The model's performance metrics showed accuracy above 90%. Sensitivity and specificity both exceeded benchmarks. The software vendor provided documentation demonstrating that the algorithm had been validated on datasets larger than any single radiologist would encounter in a career. Her anecdotal observations, though noted, were insufficient to challenge deployment decisions made at considerable expense. As a result, additional training was arranged to encourage radiologists to review scans independently and to remain alert to subtle findings that might not meet the system's detection thresholds.

She stopped raising it after that. But she did not stop noticing.

The Atrophy Problem

Tools that provide answers before questions form create a specific kind of dependency. The answer arrives so quickly that the process of working towards it never develops. A student who uses a calculator for every arithmetic problem never builds fluency with numbers. A driver who relies on GPS for every journey never develops spatial awareness. A professional who accepts AI outputs without interrogating them never builds the judgement to recognise when those outputs have gone wrong.

The capability withers from disuse. A radiologist who spent fifteen years reading scans without assistance retains interpretive skill for years after the overlay arrives, because the foundation was laid when learning required it. A radiologist who learns with the overlay in place never builds that foundation, because the tool removes the friction that drives skill formation.

Marcus saw this in his own work. Junior developers who had learned to code with AI assistance could quickly produce working code. They understood syntax, recognised common patterns, and could debug errors flagged by the IDE. They struggled, however, with architectural decisions that required understanding how different parts of a system would interact under conditions the code had not yet encountered. They had never built the mental models that come from writing code slowly, making mistakes, and tracing those mistakes through layers of logic until the source grows clear.

The tool had made them faster. It had not made them better at the parts of the work that tools could not do.

Maintaining What Markets Ignore

Sarah's weekly practice of reading scans without the overlay had turned into something she could barely justify to herself. It took time she could not bill. It produced no measurable benefit. The work was redundant by definition.

Yet she continued because she understood what would happen if she stopped. The fluency developed through years of independent practice would fade. Her eyes would stop moving across the image in the way they once had. She would start waiting for the overlay, like everyone else, and once she did, she could no longer work without it.

On a Thursday afternoon in November, the hospital's network went down for four hours. The diagnostic system was offline. The queue continued to grow. Newer radiologists waited, refreshing their screens periodically, hoping the system would return. Sarah kept working. She opened scans without the overlay because she had never stopped knowing how. By the time the network came back, she had cleared a third of the backlog herself, while her colleagues had processed nothing.

No one noticed. The metrics that mattered to the hospital showed a temporary slowdown, then a recovery. Sarah's contribution appeared nowhere in the reports.

Deliberate Difficulty

Maintaining cognitive capability under automation pressure requires accepting inefficiency that institutions punish. It requires doing work the hard way when the easy way is available. A translator who wants to maintain fluency in a language while working with real-time translation tools must occasionally translate without them. A designer who seeks to maintain spatial reasoning while using generative layout tools must occasionally sketch by hand. A programmer who wants to maintain architectural judgement while working with code generation must occasionally write the code from scratch.

The practice appears wasteful by every measure of efficiency. It produces output that could have been produced faster. It takes time that could have been spent on higher-value work. It looks like opposition to progress.

Yet it is the only way to prevent the capability from disappearing entirely. Once the capability is gone, it cannot be rebuilt quickly. A radiologist who has spent five years relying entirely on diagnostic overlays cannot suddenly read scans independently when the system fails. The knowledge remains in an abstract sense, but the fluency is lost.

When Convenience Becomes a Trap

Marcus tried an experiment in March. He spent one week writing code without using the AI assistant that had become standard in his workflow. No autocomplete suggestions. No generated boilerplate. No explanations of library functions he had forgotten. Just the documentation, the compiler, and his own knowledge.

The first day was frustrating. His fingers kept pausing, waiting for suggestions that did not come. Simple tasks took twice as long. He found himself reaching for the assistant repeatedly, then stopping himself, then realising how dependent he had grown on it for things he once knew automatically.

By the third day, something shifted. His thinking slowed, but deepened. Without suggestions appearing instantly, he had to hold more context in his head. He had to remember how the different parts of the software architecture connected. He had to think through implications before writing code, because fixing mistakes later would be more expensive without the tool to catch them immediately.

By Friday, he understood why the junior developers struggled with architecture. They had never had to hold the whole structure in their heads because the tools broke everything into small, manageable pieces. They could implement features without understanding where those features fit within the larger system. The tools had made them productive without making them thoughtful.

Marcus returned to using the assistant the following week. But he also started blocking out time each month to work without it.

The Market Does Not Care

Sarah's hospital did not reward her for maintaining an independent diagnostic capability. Marcus's firm did not promote him for practising coding and performing code reviews without AI assistance. The market optimises for output, not for resilience. The professional who maintains capability through deliberate difficulty appears less efficient than the professional who relies entirely on tools.

This creates a trap. The professional who maintains capability sacrifices short-term efficiency for long-term resilience. The professional who relies entirely on tools gains short-term efficiency but loses long-term capability. The market rewards the second choice immediately and punishes the first choice continuously, until the moment when tools fail, and capability suddenly matters.

By then, roles that maintained independent capability have often disappeared, because the market made that approach unsustainable. Work that depended entirely on tools persists, and organisations discover too late that the capability they need cannot be rebuilt quickly.

Capability maintained against institutional pressure leaves no trace in any report. It appears nowhere in performance reviews. It produces nothing the dashboard can measure. It shows up only when everything else fails, briefly, before the moment passes and the metrics return to normal. The market does not reward that moment. It does not even see it. It simply inherits the consequences when the people who sustained it are gone.

INITIATED BY AI

12

THE RIGHT TO THINK

Consider a thought experiment drawn from current debates in higher education. It is used here not as a report on a specific institution, but as a simplified model that clarifies dynamics already under discussion across universities.

A language department requires all students to use an AI writing assistant for their coursework. The intention is good. The consequence is not. The stated goal is fairness. If everyone has access to the same tools, the argument goes, then everyone competes on equal ground. The assistant helps struggling writers reach acceptable standards. Academic performance improves in measurable ways.

Within two years, the language department begins to notice something unsettling. Students can produce polished essays, but many struggle to explain their own arguments when questioned. They generate sophisticated analysis, yet falter when asked to develop ideas without the tool. They have learned to prompt, edit, and select from the options provided by the assistant. They have had less practice thinking through problems from first principles.

A professor runs an exercise. She assigns an essay, collects the submissions, then calls students in individually and asks them to explain their core arguments without notes or screens. Many cannot do so. Their names appear on the documents, but much of the reasoning process has been shaped by the tool.

The department then revises its policy the following year. Use of the assistant is no longer required. Some students continue to rely on it. Others reduce their use. The division becomes apparent in upper-level seminars, where discussion reveals who has developed independent analytical capability and who has become dependent on tools to structure their thinking.

This thought experiment illustrates cognitive liberty by showing what happens when the starting point of thinking shifts from the person to the tool. Students still produce polished work, but the initiation of reasoning no longer reliably begins in their own mental process. Their ability to reason from first principles begins to fade. They become proficient at using the tool, but their capacity to think without it diminishes, not because they lack intelligence, but because the conditions that once required independent reasoning are no longer present. Cognitive liberty concerns the capacity to direct attention, frame problems independently, and generate lines of thought that are not pre-structured by a system. In this example, the tool shapes the space in which ideas emerge, thereby narrowing intellectual movement. What is at stake is not the quality of output, but the preservation of independent cognitive agency.

The Right to Think Slowly

Cognitive liberty is the capacity to develop thoughts without external structures shaping them before they form. It concerns preserving the space in which independent thinking can occur before tools arrive to assist or direct.

This space is shrinking. Search engines supply answers before questions are fully formed. Autocomplete finishes sentences before writers know what they want to say. Recommendation algorithms curate information before readers decide what interests them. Each intervention removes a moment where thought could have developed independently.

The interventions are helpful. They save time, reduce friction, and often improve outcomes. Yet they also reshape the process of thinking itself, shifting it from struggle-formed judgement to selection among pre-generated options. That shift is not neutral. It is a loss that compounds quietly until independent thought becomes structurally impractical.

Where Persuasion Becomes Direction

While waiting to enter the profession, Aisha spent two years volunteering as a technical editor for an open-source documentation platform that tracked engagement metrics in real time. The dashboard showed which articles were being read, how long readers stayed, and which topics generated the most return visits. The data was genuinely useful. It revealed what practitioners actually cared about rather than what editors assumed they cared about.

But it also changed what she commissioned. Writers pitched pieces that resembled those that had performed well previously.

She approved pieces that fit established patterns because the data validated the choice. Coverage narrowed towards topics the algorithm had learnt to recognise as engaging, and away from the kind of structural analysis she had built her own writing practice around.

She was still making editorial decisions. The data was one input among many. Yet that one input carried disproportionate weight because it was quantified, comparable, and updated continuously. A writer arguing for a piece that did not fit the pattern found herself arguing against data, which felt like arguing against reality.

The direction was subtle. Nobody told Aisha what to commission. The dashboard made certain kinds of pieces easier to justify than others. The space for work that did not fit established patterns was narrowed through many small decisions that each felt reasonable at the time.

What eroded was not the act of deciding, but the freedom to decide what deserved attention in the first place. Aisha recognised this only when she noticed that the questions she was no longer commissioning were the ones she had most wanted to ask when she started.

When Algorithms Know What You Want

While working on her blog and editing for the platform, Aisha noticed the same narrowing in her own media consumption. The articles in her feed were relevant, well-written, and aligned with her interests. She rarely encountered content that challenged her assumptions because the algorithm had learnt what kept her engaged.

She tried an experiment. For one month, she turned off all

recommendation settings and navigated the apps manually. She followed links, browsed categories, and read articles chosen for reasons beyond algorithmic suggestions. The experience was disorienting. Much of what she found was irrelevant or poorly written. Occasionally, she encountered viewpoints that irritated her enough to stop reading.

But she also encountered ideas she would never have found through recommendations. Some of these ideas changed how she thought about problems she had been working on in her blog. They introduced perspectives she had not considered because the algorithm had correctly judged that they would not keep her engaged.

By the end of the month, Aisha understood that optimisation for engagement was also optimisation for intellectual stagnation. The algorithm gave her what she wanted in the short-term while quietly narrowing what she could discover in the long-term.

Preserving the Mess

Thinking is not efficient. It involves false starts, dead ends, and extended periods where nothing useful appears to be happening. It requires holding contradictions without resolving them immediately, exploring directions that may prove fruitless, and tolerating uncertainty long enough for patterns to emerge organically.

Tools optimise thinking by removing the mess. They provide structure before you have determined what you want to say. They generate options before you have decided what you are trying to achieve. They resolve uncertainty before you have sat with it long enough to understand what it means.

The efficiency is real, and the cost is harder to see, which makes it more rather than less important to defend the conditions under which thinking develops slowly. The cost takes the form of thoughts that never develop and connections that never form, because the space where they might have emerged has been filled before they could.

Sarah preserved the space for independent diagnostic thinking, at a cost the hospital never measured and would not have rewarded. The preservation required accepting that some of her thinking would yield no useful results. Some scans would be exactly as the overlay suggested. Some of her independent observations would be wrong. The practice was valuable not because it always produced better answers, but because it maintained the capacity to produce answers independently when circumstances required it.

When Choice Requires the Environment

A student who learns to write only with AI assistance has not lost the ability to write independently. They never developed it. What they have lost is the environment that enables independent writing. This includes the patience to work through a problem slowly, the tolerance for sentences that fail on the first attempt, and the willingness to delete paragraphs that seemed promising but led nowhere.

That environment must be preserved for students to practise. Practice means writing badly for long enough that writing well eventually becomes possible. Tools that eliminate bad writing also eliminate the process by which foundational capacity is formed. The student can still produce good writing, but only with the tool present. Remove the tool, and they lack not just the skill but the foundational capacity to develop it.

This is why formal freedom is insufficient. The student may choose to write independently, but that option is not available because the prerequisites for independent work were not established. What appears to be a free choice between using tools and not using them is actually a choice between using tools and producing nothing.

Cognitive liberty requires more than the formal right to think independently. It requires preserving the conditions that allow independent thought to develop. Institutions that mandate the use of tools eliminate those conditions. Markets that reward efficiency eliminate the time and the opportunity needed for those conditions to exist. The capability atrophies not through prohibition but through a structure that makes its development impractical.

What Cannot Be Delegated

Some forms of thinking cannot be outsourced without fundamentally changing what they produce. Moral reasoning requires working through implications that do not resolve cleanly. Creative insight requires holding contradictions until something new emerges. Strategic judgement requires integrating information that eludes formal analysis.

Tools can assist these processes. They cannot replace them. A tool can generate arguments, but cannot determine which ones matter in context. It can produce options but cannot weigh them against values that resist quantification. And it cannot recognise when the frame defining what counts as information has itself become the problem.

Sarah's diagnostic work involved this kind of irreducible

judgement. She could use the overlay. She could not delegate the decision about whether to trust the overlay's display. That decision required integrating the algorithmic output with clinical intuition, patient history, and awareness of edge cases where established categories did not apply.

As tools grow more sophisticated, the temptation to delegate this judgement must be resisted. The tool's output looks more authoritative. The effort required to evaluate it independently feels increasingly wasteful. The market rewards those who accept tool outputs quickly, rather than those who interrogate them carefully.

Yet the judgement stays necessary. AI models fail in ways their designers did not anticipate. Contexts shift in ways that algorithms trained on historical data cannot recognise. Values evolve in ways that make yesterday's optimisation today's harm. Someone must preserve the ability to recognise when outputs that appear correct are actually incorrect.

Cognitive liberty defends against a future in which independent thought becomes structurally impractical, not through prohibition but through conditions that make its development impossible for most.

13

THE STRUCTURES OF INFLUENCE

Where Decisions Happen

Decisions about the use of technology are made at points where authority is concentrated. These points are situated within organisational hierarchies, procurement processes, and regulatory frameworks. Most workers never get to participate in the decision-making process. By the time the technology reaches the people who will use it, the meaningful choices have already been made.

The Australian bank where the customer service lead had worked purchased customer relationship management software through a procurement process managed by the finance department. The evaluation criteria focus on cost, vendor reputation, regulatory compliance, and integration with existing systems. Data accuracy matters, but it competes with other priorities. Customer service representatives who will rely on the software participate in surveys and feedback sessions held after the shortlist is established and the finalists selected.

The choice is constrained by what procurement and IT processes deem acceptable. Representatives can express preferences, raise concerns, and request modifications, but the frame within which the decision operates is already set.

Sarah experienced the same dynamic in her hospital when her department raised concerns about the tendency of diagnostic overlays to miss early-stage nodules. The hospital administration took the feedback seriously and scheduled a meeting with the software vendor. The vendor acknowledged the issue, explained that it was a known limitation of the current model version, and committed to improvements in the next release. The hospital accepted this response, and the overlay stayed in production. The next release arrived eighteen months later with incremental improvements that did not address the fundamental problem Sarah had identified.

The power to raise concerns is not the same as the power to stop deployment. The first operates at the level of feedback. The second operates at the level of authority.

Veto Points and Friction

Political scientists use the term veto point to describe moments in a decision-making process in which a single actor can block an outcome. Constitutional structures create veto points deliberately. A proposal often needs approval from more than one decision-making body. A rule may be subject to legal challenge before it takes effect. An agreement may require formal approval before it becomes binding. These points distribute power by requiring multiple parties to agree before significant changes can proceed.

In most organisations, technology deployment has few veto

points. The decision to adopt a system typically requires approval from budget holders, compliance officers, and technical leadership. It rarely requires approval from the workers who will use it. This asymmetry allows deployment to proceed rapidly once the relevant authorities align, regardless of whether the people most affected by the technology agree.

A logistics company in Manchester deployed route-optimisation software in 2023 following a six-month evaluation by the operations team. The software reduced fuel costs by 8% and improved delivery intervals by 6%. Drivers reported that the routes were often impractical, with unrealistic timelines and a disregard for local knowledge of traffic patterns, loading zone availability, and customer preferences. The drivers raised these concerns using the company's feedback channels. Management reviewed the feedback and determined that the efficiency gains outweighed the operational friction reported by the drivers. The operating model stayed in place. Driver turnover increased by 24% over the following year. The company responded by increasing recruitment and streamlining onboarding, treating turnover as a staffing problem rather than a technology problem. Drivers had a voice but not power. They could describe the issues. They could not compel change. The veto point sat elsewhere in the organisation, held by people who measured different outcomes and responded to different pressures.

Where Leverage Exists

Union representation creates a veto point by establishing a legal requirement for consultation before certain decisions can proceed. The union cannot always prevent deployment, but it can impose costs on moving forward without agreement. Delay is expensive. Conflict is disruptive. The possibility of both creates an incentive to negotiate.

Unions have negotiated different forms of advance notice. Works councils in Germany have secured agreements requiring consultation before major automation decisions. The International Longshore and Warehouse Union negotiated a technology clause in its Pacific Coast contract that requires advance notice before automation that could affect jobs is deployed. Neither agreement gave workers the power to block deployment, but both created time for assessment by requiring six months' notice before any automation that might affect employment could proceed. The notice period did not confer veto power. Still, it created intervals for assessment, for questions to be asked, for alternatives to be proposed, and for evidence to be gathered about whether the technology performed as promised.

Six months is not long. It is sufficient for problems to surface. A system that looks promising in testing may reveal limitations when exposed to real-world conditions. A vendor's claims may prove optimistic. An algorithm that performs well in controlled environments may fail as variability increases. The notice period creates a window during which these realities can emerge before the organisation commits to dependencies that it cannot easily reverse.

Professional standards operate similarly. Medical licensing boards can require that diagnostic systems meet specific performance thresholds before physicians are permitted to rely on them in clinical practice. Architectural review boards can mandate that structural analysis software be verified by licensed engineers before designs proceed to construction. Legal bar associations can stipulate that contract analysis tools must preserve attorney oversight of final decisions.

These standards do not prevent the adoption of technology. They establish conditions under which adoption can occur safely. The conditions create friction, which slows deployment and creates intervals for evaluation, sometimes revealing problems that would otherwise have been discovered only after the technology was embedded and removal had become prohibitively expensive.

Regulatory Capture

Leverage arises when regulation imposes requirements that technology must satisfy before deployment. The quality of that leverage depends on who writes the regulations and whose interests they serve.

Regulatory capture refers to the process by which the entities being regulated gain control over the regulatory process itself. The outcome is a regulation that appears to constrain behaviour while actually protecting incumbent interests. It often creates compliance costs that function as barriers to entry, advantaging large firms that can afford them while excluding smaller competitors.

AI regulation faces this risk acutely. The companies developing AI possess resources, expertise, and political access that workers and civil society groups lack. When governments convene advisory committees to develop AI governance frameworks, the committees are often dominated by representatives from technology companies, industry associations, and academic institutions with close ties to the industry. The regulations that emerge from these processes tend to favour approaches favoured by technology companies: voluntary standards, self-certification, and principles-based frameworks that maximise flexibility.

These approaches are not necessarily wrong. They may be appropriate for rapidly evolving technologies, where rigid rules would quickly become obsolete. But they also create environments in which deployment proceeds with minimal friction, companies set their own standards, and enforcement depends on trust rather than verification.

A worker attempting to challenge an algorithmic decision in such an environment confronts a structure designed by people who benefit from the deployment proceeding smoothly.

Transparency as Precondition

Influence depends on access to information. A worker cannot challenge an algorithmic decision if they do not know it has been made. A professional cannot contest a performance metric they have never been shown. A union cannot negotiate over an operating model it learns about only after deployment is complete.

Transparency alone is insufficient for influence, but opacity makes influence impossible. If deployment proceeds in secret, if algorithms operate without explanation, if decisions cannot be traced to their origins, then contestation grows impossible regardless of what formal rights exist.

The European Union's General Data Protection Regulation limits purely automated decisions that have legal or similarly significant effects, requiring that affected individuals be informed and afforded safeguards, such as human review and the ability to contest the decision. While this provision has sometimes been described as a "right to explanation," GDPR does not create a universal entitlement to full algorithmic disclosure in every context. The regulation requires organisations to provide meaningful information about the logic involved, but it does not specify what constitutes an adequate explanation or require the disclosure of proprietary algorithms. The definition of "similarly significant" leaves room for interpretation. Enforcement is inconsistent.

Yet the principle matters. It establishes that opacity is unacceptable, that systems that affect people's lives must be legible, and that those affected by decisions have a right to understand how those decisions were made. The principle creates a basis for challenge that would not exist if the regulation accepted that AI systems are too complex to explain.

Sarah's hospital deployed diagnostic AI without explaining to its radiologists how the model weighted different imaging features or where its detection thresholds had been set. When she raised concerns about early-stage nodules being missed, she could not trace the limitation to its source because the model's logic was not visible to her. Under GDPR, the hospital would have been required to provide meaningful information about the logic involved. That information would have allowed her to identify whether the problem was a threshold setting, a training data gap, or a structural limitation of the model. Without it, she could describe the symptom but could not diagnose the cause.

Collective Action

Individual workers can raise concerns, refuse to cooperate, and resign in protest. These actions carry personal cost and seldom alter institutional behaviour on their own. Sarah objected to the limitations of the overlays and was offered additional training.

Marcus argued for human review in the deployment loop and was told the firm could not afford the delay. The overlay stayed. The deployment continued. Their individual objections changed nothing structural.

Collective action changes the calculation. A radiology department that objects collectively can halt deployment by refusing to validate the apparatus's outputs. A warehouse where workers coordinate a slowdown can impose costs that make algorithmic management impractical. A professional association that threatens to decertify a practice can force institutions to reconsider deployment decisions.

The power is structural rather than individual. An organisation can replace one worker. It cannot easily replace an entire department, workforce, or professional community. The capacity to act collectively creates leverage that individuals lack.

That capacity depends on the organisation, which takes time to build and requires coordination across workers who may have competing interests. It hinges on legal protections that allow collective action without immediate retaliation. It depends on the solidarity that can withstand the pressure that institutions apply when their authority is challenged.

These conditions exist unevenly. Some workers have unions. Others work in contexts where organising is difficult or illegal. Some professions have strong associations that can enforce standards. Others operate in fragmented industries where coordination is nearly impossible. The distribution of collective power determines who has leverage to shape deployment and who must accept the operating model imposed on them.

Where Marcus Could Not Reach

Marcus preserved capability through deliberate practice. He built recognition beyond his current employer. Yet he could not modify the competitive dynamics that forced his firm to adopt AI systems faster than he could evaluate them.

The deployment meeting in March made that clear. The code review process was decided by people who don't write code daily, using criteria that excluded the judgement of those who would depend on it, and consultation was treated as optional.

Marcus had a say but lacked a veto. He could raise concerns. He could not stop the deployment. The structure of authority in his organisation concentrated decision-making power at coordination points where developers had representation but not control.

This is not an accident. Organisations are deliberately designed this way to enable efficient decision-making without requiring consensus from everyone affected. The design serves legitimate purposes. It also creates vulnerability for workers whose expertise matters but whose preferences do not determine outcomes.

Personal strategies create individual resilience. They do not alter the institutional structures that determine how and when technology gets deployed. Those structures either respond to collective pressure or do not respond at all.

Sarah maintained her diagnostic independence. The hospital continued to deploy systems that made independence more difficult to sustain. Marcus preserved his architectural judgement. His firm continued accelerating deployment in ways that made that judgement less relevant. Aisha built public recognition. The profession she entered continued to automate in ways that raised the barriers she had worked to overcome.

The trap remains because the structures of influence operate above the level at which individual responses can operate. Understanding where these structures concentrate, where veto points lie, and where collective leverage can be employed does not offer an escape. Instead, it clarifies what is needed to change the conditions rather than simply adapting to them.

14

HUMAN ACCOUNTABILITY

The autonomous vehicle struck a pedestrian in Tempe, Arizona, in March 2018. The car was operating in self-driving mode. A safety driver sat behind the wheel, monitoring the system in accordance with the manufacturer's protocols. The vehicle's sensors detected the pedestrian but misclassified her as a false positive. The braking system did not engage. The safety driver, who had been watching a television show on her phone, looked up too late to intervene.

The pedestrian died. The question that followed was straightforward: who was responsible?

There was no clean answer. The vehicle's software failed to respond appropriately. The safety driver failed to monitor attentively. The manufacturer failed to ensure the operating model performed safely. The state failed to regulate adequately. Responsibility diffused across so many parties that prosecuting any single one felt arbitrary.

Eventually, charges were filed against the safety driver. She was held accountable for failing to supervise an operating model designed to function without supervision, installed in a vehicle marketed as autonomous, and tested on public roads under regulations that assumed human oversight remained meaningful.

The decision to prosecute the driver resolved the legal question while leaving the structural question untouched. When AI acts first, and humans respond second, who bears responsibility for the outcome?

The Accountability Gap

Traditional accountability operates on a simple principle. The person who makes a decision bears responsibility for its effects. A doctor who prescribes the wrong medication is accountable for the harm that follows. A pilot who misjudges a landing is accountable for the crash. An engineer who designs a bridge that collapses is accountable for the failure.

AI disrupts this logic by separating the decision from the human response. The system acts first. The human confirms, adjusts, or overrides. When outcomes are poor, accountability becomes unclear. Did the human fail by trusting the system? Did the system fail by providing flawed guidance? Did the organisation fail by deploying an operating model that was not ready? Did the regulator fail by permitting deployment under inadequate standards?

In practice, accountability flows downward to the person in the lowest position within the hierarchy with formal authority. The safety driver is held liable because she was physically present and legally responsible. The radiologist gets sued because her signature appears on the report. The hiring manager is held responsible for the final selection from the shortlist generated by the algorithm.

This resolution serves institutional interests. It places blame on someone who can be removed, disciplined, or prosecuted. It protects the organisation, the technology company, and the regulatory framework from questions about whether the structure itself created conditions that made failure likely.

Yet it does nothing to prevent the same failure from recurring, because the structural conditions that produced it remain unchanged.

When Oversight Becomes Theatre

Sarah signed every diagnostic report issued by the hospital. Her signature made her legally responsible for the report's conclusions. Yet by the time she signed, the examination had followed paths the overlay suggested. The red boxes had highlighted what mattered. The confidence scores indicated the system's certainty. Her role was verification, not initiation.

Legally, that distinction did not matter. If the diagnosis was wrong and harm resulted, Sarah would be accountable. The hospital would point to her signature. The medical licensing board would review her decision. The legal framework would treat her as if she had conducted the entire examination independently.

This creates a form of accountability theatre in which formal responsibility rests with humans while practical authority has shifted elsewhere. The human remains in the loop to absorb liability. The system makes the substantive decisions. It protects institutions while leaving professionals exposed.

A similar pattern appeared in financial services after the 2008 crisis. Banks adopted algorithmic trading systems that executed thousands of decisions per second. When trades went wrong and losses mounted, firms argued that the traders monitoring the systems were responsible for failing to intervene. Traders countered that the systems operated too quickly for meaningful oversight and that their employers had encouraged reliance on automated execution.

The legal resolution was predictable. Some traders were dismissed, some were fined, and a few were prosecuted. The systems remained in place. The operating model that made effective oversight impractical, even though it was legally required, remained unchanged.

The Speed Problem

Human accountability assumes that people can evaluate decisions within timeframes that allow harm to be prevented. That assumption fails when systems operate faster than human judgement can function.

An algorithmic trading system can execute thousands of transactions in the time it takes a human to read a single screen. A content moderation system can review millions of posts while a human moderator is still logging in. A fraud detection system can block accounts faster than a customer service representative can answer the phone.

Speed is the point. These systems exist because human-paced decision-making is too slow for the scale at which digital platforms operate. Yet that same speed makes accountability impossible. You cannot hold someone accountable for failing to prevent something they could not have prevented.

Organisations respond by treating speed as a natural constraint rather than a design choice. They argue that meaningful human oversight would make the operating model impractical, as though that resolves the issue rather than raising it. If human oversight is impractical, the system may be unsuitable for contexts in which accountability is essential.

The counter-argument is genuine. A fraud detection system that cannot block suspicious transactions immediately would enable theft. A moderation system that cannot respond to viral content within minutes would allow harm to spread. Slowing these systems creates different harms.

These arguments are not wrong. They demonstrate that some contexts are incompatible with human accountability. Once that incompatibility is acknowledged, the question shifts. Do the benefits of automation justify accepting outcomes for which no one can be held responsible for prevention?

When No One Designed the Outcome

Who is accountable when the algorithm rejects a qualified candidate because they attended the wrong institution?

The recruiter did not design the bias. They used the company-provided tool. The data scientist who built the algorithm did not intend to induce bias. They trained the model on data provided by the company. The company did not deliberately create the bias. It emerged from historical decisions made by people who are no longer there.

The outcome has no author. It emerged from a process in which many people made reasonable local decisions that produced an unreasonable collective outcome. No individual decision created bias. The structure as a whole gave rise to it.

Accountability frameworks struggle with emergent outcomes. Legal processes seek intent, decisions that can be traced to specific people. Hiring bias has no single point of origin. It is the predictable result of a process, yet no individual within that process can be held solely accountable for it.

Organisations respond by treating algorithmic outcomes as natural phenomena rather than the result of design. They acknowledge that bias exists, commit to addressing it in future versions, and continue using the current system while improvements are developed. The commitment is sincere. It also ensures that no one is held responsible for the harm the present system continues to produce.

Distributed Responsibility

If a medical AI system misses a diagnosis, Sarah or the radiologist who verified the scan is held professionally and legally accountable. Yet responsibility is distributed across multiple parties whose decisions collectively produced the failure.

The software company designed an algorithm that prioritised sensitivity over specificity, increasing false negatives. The hospital purchased the software after an evaluation that prioritised cost over clinical performance. The training data contained biases that the model learned and amplified. The regulatory framework permitted deployment without requiring validation across diverse populations. The radiologist trusted the system because everyone around her trusted it, and questioning it would have made her appear incompetent.

Each party made reasonable decisions within the constraints they faced. The software company optimised for the metrics that mattered most to customers. The hospital worked within budget limitations. The training data reflected available information. The regulatory framework balanced innovation against caution. The radiologist followed professional norms.

The collective result was a missed diagnosis. No single

decision caused it, but the combination produced it. Holding the radiologist accountable serves no purpose, as her decisions were reasonable given the environment in which she worked. The environment was constructed by choices made elsewhere, by people who will never be held accountable for the missed diagnosis.

When Markets Determine Liability

Technology companies structure their relationships with customers to minimise liability. Licensing agreements specify that the software is provided "as is" without guarantees of performance. Liability clauses cap damages at amounts far below the potential harm the software might cause. Arbitration requirements prevent customers from bringing class-action suits or pursuing claims in court.

These terms are standard in software licensing. They shift risk from the company that designs the system to the organisation that deploys it and ultimately to the workers who use it. When something goes wrong, the company can point to the licensing terms. The organisation can point to the worker who was formally responsible. The worker has nowhere to point. Neither does the department head who approved the protocol, the administrator who signed the procurement contract, or the IT director who managed the implementation. The licensing terms protect one party only. Everyone else in the chain absorbs the risk proportional to where their signature appears.

This arrangement appears to work for technology companies. It distributes accountability across everyone who touched the process while protecting the one party with the greatest power to have designed it differently. Yet the structure creates a problem for everyone in the chain. When accountability diffuses downward and foreseeable failures go unaddressed, trust erodes. Organisations become reluctant to deploy. Professionals become reluctant to rely on systems that expose them to liability they cannot control. The technology company that structured its agreements to avoid accountability ultimately operates in a market made smaller by the distrust its structure produced. Better accountability frameworks are not a constraint on the industry. They are a condition for its long term viability.

What Changes the Calculation

Collective mechanisms do not just protect workers. They change where accountability lands. A professional association that requires validation before members can use a diagnostic system forces the accountability question upstream, onto the company that must now demonstrate the system performs as claimed. A union that negotiates liability protection for workers who follow algorithmic recommendations shifts exposure away from the individual who signed the report towards the institution that mandated the process.

None of these mechanisms eliminates risk. They change who bears it. Instead of concentrating risk on the individual worker who signs the report or approves the decision, they distribute it across the parties with real power to shape how the system operates.

A European regulation passed in 2024 requires that AI systems used in high-risk contexts maintain human oversight and that the organisation deploying the system be held liable for harms that result from inadequate oversight. The regulation does not eliminate individual accountability; rather, it establishes that institutions cannot use algorithms to shield themselves from responsibility for the outcomes their systems produce.

The regulation is imperfect. Defining "high-risk contexts" leaves room for interpretation. Establishing causation between system failure and harm is difficult. Enforcement hinges on regulatory capacity, which varies across member states. Nevertheless, the principle holds. It establishes that deploying AI does not eliminate institutional accountability and that workers cannot be made solely responsible for outcomes they did not fully control.

Where Accountability Must Land

Marcus cannot be held accountable for architectural decisions made by automated deployment systems he did not design and cannot override. Sarah cannot be held accountable for diagnostic conclusions that follow directly from algorithmic highlighting she is professionally required to trust. Aisha cannot be held accountable for meeting hiring criteria that change based on models she never sees and cannot influence.

Yet current frameworks assign responsibility as if these conditions did not exist. The programmer signs the code review. The radiologist signs the report. The candidate accepts the rejection. The legal system treats these signatures as if they were autonomous decisions rather than confirmations of outcomes that had been substantially determined before the human entered the process.

Accountability that ignores how authority actually operates becomes a mechanism for protecting institutions while exposing workers. The doctor is being sued. The hospital points to its compliance procedures. The software company points to its licensing terms. The regulator points to the standards that were followed. Responsibility diffuses everywhere except to the parties with the power to change the arrangement.

This preserves the appearance of accountability without substance. Professionals remain formally responsible, while the practical authority to prevent harm shifts elsewhere.

Real accountability requires responsibility to align with authority. Those who design systems must be accountable for foreseeable failures. Those who deploy systems must be accountable for providing adequate oversight. Those who profit from automation must bear the costs when it harms.

Workers should be accountable for their judgement within constraints, not for the constraints themselves.

The safety driver in Arizona was prosecuted for failing to supervise a system designed to function without her. The legal system found its answer but the structural question was never asked. The manufacturer continued operating and the regulatory framework remained unchanged. The operating model that made meaningful oversight impractical stayed in place. The same logic now operates in hospitals, warehouses, banks, and engineering firms. Who bears responsibility when the system acts first and the human signs second? The structures being built now will answer that question. The answer will determine whether accountability means something real or whether it simply means finding the person closest to the harm and making them carry it alone.

15

WHAT REMAINS HUMAN

What makes work human is not that humans do it. It is that humans decide where it begins, what questions it asks, and what forms of attention it elicits. When those decisions shift elsewhere, the character of the work changes, even when the tasks remain the same.

A violinist spent sixty years mastering her instrument. By the time she turned seventy, she could make the violin sing in ways that moved audiences to tears. The control was absolute. The expression was profound. She had devoted her life to this singular pursuit, and devotion showed in every note.

Then someone developed software that could replicate her playing with remarkable accuracy. It analysed the physics of her bowing technique, the precise finger placements, and the tiny timing variations that created emotional resonance. It could perform pieces she had recorded, and in controlled tests, many listeners could not distinguish the software from the original.

The violinist was asked what she thought about this development. She smiled and said the software had missed the point entirely.

The performance was not what mattered. The performance was simply evidence of what mattered: the decades of practice, the thousands of hours spent working through passages that would not resolve, the frustration and tedium, and the occasional moments of breakthrough that shaped not just her playing but her character.

The software could produce the output. It could not experience the process that made the output meaningful.

What Cannot Be Replicated

Within the shift already described, AI challenges each capacity that once defined human uniqueness. Tools now make better tools than we do. Planning happens faster through simulation than through human deliberation. Abstract reasoning operates at scales we cannot match. Meaning-making itself begins to resemble pattern recognition, which algorithms handle efficiently.

If capacity defines humanity and capacity proves replicable, then what remains human? Sarah's thirty-minute scan practice was inefficient. It was also irreducibly hers. The hospital could replace her diagnostic accuracy with a more capable algorithm, but it could not replace the deliberate effort she invested in maintaining capability against institutional pressure. That effort expressed something algorithms cannot replicate: the choice to preserve capability that markets no longer value.

The Burden of Autonomy

Automation removes burdens. It makes work easier, faster, and more reliable. A surgeon assisted by robotic precision makes incisions that human hands cannot achieve. A pilot guided by autopilot manages emergencies with composure that stress would otherwise compromise. A diagnostician, guided by pattern recognition, detects diseases at stages when intervention is still effective. These benefits are real, and denying them would be dishonest.

The technology addresses genuine human frailty. We tire after hours of concentration. Our attention drifts under monotony. Hunger, stress, and fatigue degrade judgement in ways we cannot fully compensate for through discipline alone. Bias shapes perception before conscious thought can intervene. AI operates without these limitations, maintaining consistency across conditions that reduce human performance to chance.

Yet the burdens that disappear often carried something worth preserving: the experience of struggling against adversity, the satisfaction of overcoming obstacles, the development of character through unavoidable challenges. The surgeon who never operates without robotic assistance loses the tactile sense that catches complications before instruments register them. The pilot who relies on autopilot for routine operations finds manual control unfamiliar when systems fail. The diagnostician who begins with AI flagging develops habits of attention that function only when the system operates as expected.

The professional who never works without tools is spared inefficiency. They are also spared the confidence that comes from knowing their capability persists independently.

Autonomy is a burden. Dependence is easier. The question is not whether to accept assistance but whether to preserve the capacity for autonomy even when dependence would suffice.

What AI Does Well

Marcus remained after the restructuring because losing him would have disrupted coordination. That value existed regardless of whether the metrics captured it. The metrics measured output. The value resided in relationships, context, and effect that eluded quantification.

Markets optimise for what they can measure. They systematically miss what measurements cannot reach. Markets cannot measure our limitations, nor can they measure what we lose when those limitations disappear.

The advantages AI brings are real, categorical, and compounding. They are not improvements in degree but differences in kind that change who decides, where judgement begins, and what human expertise can still contribute.

AI operates at scales humans cannot match. A radiologist reviews 200 scans a day, maintaining focus through effort and experience that degrade under fatigue. An AI system processes 200,000 scans across a hospital network in the same period, maintaining perfect consistency and detecting patterns across dimensions that no individual can hold in mind simultaneously. This is not an efficiency gain. It is a categorical difference that shifts what counts as viable professional practice.

The scale changes what becomes possible to know. Fraud patterns that span continents, time frames, and behavioural signals emerge from correlations no human analyst could perceive. Early disease indicators appear as a constellation of weak medical signals that no clinician would recognise as connected. Market movements derive from interactions between variables that intuition cannot integrate. These patterns are not subtle versions of what experts already notice. They are relationships that exist only at scales beyond human attention.

Consistency matters where variation creates risk. Humans drift by mood, fatigue, hunger, and context in ways that training cannot fully eliminate. Bias shapes perception before conscious thought intervenes. Attention narrows under stress. Performance degrades across the day in patterns that professionals learn to compensate for but cannot prevent. AI applies the same criteria every time. It does not tire, does not experience emotional fluctuation, and does not selectively ignore edge cases because the hour is late or the workload is overwhelming. Once deployed, it produces the same judgement under conditions that reduce human reliability to chance.

AI acts before humans would know to act. It flags anomalies before damage occurs, redirects attention before a professional has begun, and prestructures choices before conscious judgement starts. The system determines which scan receives attention first, which transaction triggers review, and which application reaches a hiring manager. By the time human judgement begins, AI has already filtered possibilities, ranked priorities, and structured the decision space. The decision space has already been shaped. What human judgement encounters is not the full picture but the portion the system has chosen to present. Initiation has shifted upstream. Human decision-making becomes secondary rather than primary.

The learning curves diverge. A professional develops expertise over the years through cases encountered, mistakes corrected, and patterns recognised through repetition. An AI system updates its model with every interaction across the network. A diagnostic algorithm learns from every scan processed across 1,000 hospitals simultaneously, incorporating feedback at scales no individual career can match. The refinement is continuous, the scope is global, and the accumulation is permanent. Human expertise improves in steps. AI continues to improve, and the gap widens with each iteration.

Coordination costs collapse. Organisations invest substantial effort in aligning people across functions, geographies, and priorities. Meetings negotiate trade-offs. Politics delay decisions. Misalignment creates friction that limits speed and compounds error. AI coordinates actions instantly. Supply chains reroute without discussion. Resource allocation adjusts without negotiation. Workflow adapts without requiring consensus. The friction that once constrained organisational velocity disappears, and speed increases beyond what human coordination could sustain.

The economics shift irreversibly. A consultant serves one client at a time. A diagnostic algorithm serves a thousand hospitals simultaneously. Human labour scales linearly. AI scales non-linearly. Once built, an AI system can serve one user or a million at a marginal cost approaching zero. The cost curve does not bend. It collapses. This is not about efficiency. It concerns the economic structure that renders human expertise uncompetitive in contexts where scale determines viability.

Institutional memory persists in ways it never could before. Knowledge that once belonged to retiring experts now resides in systems. Judgement that took decades to develop transfers instantly. Succession planning no longer determines what the institution retains. The organisation accumulates learning across generations without depending on individuals to stay, remember, or teach. This changes the terms on which human expertise matters, because the scarcity that once made it irreplaceable has been eliminated.

These capabilities do not represent progress that preserves human contribution. They represent structural changes that redefine what human work can be. The question is not whether to pursue these advantages. Institutions that refuse them lose ground to competitors who do not. The question is whether we can structure deployment to preserve the conditions under which human judgement remains necessary, rather than becoming optional validation of conclusions reached elsewhere, and whether we will defend that necessity when the pressure to abandon it is greatest.

What Remains Possible

AI can assist with diagnosis without replacing the radiologist's ability to read a scan independently. It can suggest code without eliminating the engineer's capacity to build from first principles. The same logic applies to hiring: processing applications need not remove the manager's judgement about who would actually thrive.

These systems require deliberate design. They cost more in the short-term than full automation. They have lower throughput than systems in which AI operates without oversight.

Yet they preserve something irreplaceable. They maintain the infrastructure within which autonomous thought develops, within which professionals can still function when tools fail, and within which human judgement retains the authority to stop something when it needs to be stopped.

This future is not guaranteed. It requires choices made

now about how to structure deployment, what safeguards to maintain, and which capabilities to preserve even when markets do not reward them.

But it remains possible. The question is not whether AI eliminates human judgement. The question is whether we will design systems that preserve the necessity of judgement, create structures that preserve the capacity to question algorithmic outputs, and insist that efficiency alone does not measure value.

The tools exist to build systems that augment capability rather than replace it. The frameworks exist to require transparency, mandate review, and preserve independent verification. The knowledge exists to identify where human judgement matters most and where automation can safely proceed.

What has not yet formed is the collective will to demand these systems when speed and cost reduction point in different directions.

That will must form while choice remains. Once dependencies lock in, reversal carries costs no institution can afford. The window for building these mechanisms narrows as deployment accelerates, but it has not yet closed.

Then Governance Held

Every technology that now seems inevitable was once contested. The terms under which it operates were set by those who determined that the default was unacceptable.

In 1965, Ralph Nader published a book arguing that automobile deaths were not accidents. They were the predictable result of design decisions made by manufacturers who had calculated that safety features cost more than the litigation they would avoid. The industry response was immediate and personal. General Motors hired private investigators to follow Nader, tapped his phone, and attempted to find compromising material to discredit him. The campaign backfired. Nader sued General Motors for invasion of privacy, prevailed, and used the settlement to fund advocacy that helped push the National Traffic and Motor Vehicle Safety Act through Congress the following year, mandating safety standards the industry had long insisted were impossible.

The standards held. In the decades that followed, seat belts, airbags, and crumple zones became so routine that no one now frames road safety as a matter of individual responsibility. The frame shifted not because the industry chose to shift it, nor because drivers became more careful, but because governance changed the question asked.

Frances Kelsey joined the United States Food and Drug Administration in 1960. Her first assignment was to review a new sedative called thalidomide, already approved in forty-six countries and widely prescribed to pregnant women for morning sickness. The application looked straightforward. The manufacturer pressed for rapid approval. Kelsey was not satisfied with the evidence regarding foetal safety and refused to sign.

Her supervisors overruled her twice, but she still refused. The manufacturer contacted her superiors to demand that she be replaced. She was not replaced. In 1961, reports emerged from Europe of severe congenital disabilities in children born to mothers who had taken the drug. Thalidomide was withdrawn. Kelsey received the President's Award for Distinguished Federal Civilian Service. More consequential, the episode led to the enactment of the Kefauver-Harris Amendment of 1962, which required pharmaceutical companies to demonstrate efficacy and safety before approval rather than after harm had occurred.

The amendment changed the terms for an entire industry, permanently. One person with institutional backing, refusing to be moved, bought enough time for the evidence to surface. The institution held because it was designed to hold. Someone had previously decided that a single reviewer's judgement should be sufficient to halt a commercial process.

Aviation is the most regulated and safest mode of transport in the world. That is not a coincidence. After a series of fatal accidents in the 1970s and 1980s, aviation authorities made a structural decision: accountability would rest with systems rather than with individuals. Pilots who reported near-misses without punishment gave regulators information they could act on. Black boxes made failure legible. Checklists standardised procedures in ways that removed the discretion that exhaustion and pressure degraded. The industry did not become safer because pilots became more skilled. It became safer because the conditions under which the skill was exercised were redesigned.

These cases are not equivalent to AI. The timescales, industries, and mechanisms of harm differ. What they share is the structure of the problem: a powerful commercial interest, a diffuse and delayed harm, an argument from complexity used to resist accountability, and a political fight over who gets to set the terms. In each case, governance worked because institutions were built that could hold a line when commercial pressure pushed in the other direction.

That option is open and available. The question is whether it will be built for this technology before the window closes.

What We Already Know How to Do

Governance of powerful technologies is not a theoretical problem. It is practical, and the practice exists.

We know how to require that systems demonstrate safety before deployment rather than after harm has occurred. Pharmaceutical regulation established this principle sixty years ago. Aviation embedded it in every aspect of aircraft certification. Medical devices cannot reach clinical use without evidence. The burden of proof belongs to those who introduce the risk, not to those who bear it.

We know how to detect harm before it becomes irreversible. Aviation's near-miss reporting system works because it separates accountability for the incident from accountability for the disclosure. Pilots report because reporting is protected. Regulators learn because the information reaches them. The system accumulates knowledge faster than it accumulates harm. The same design is available for AI deployment: mandatory incident reporting, protected disclosure, and independent audit. These are not novel instruments. They are standard tools applied to a new context.

We know how to create veto points that distribute power. Works councils in Germany did not stop automation. They created intervals in which questions could be asked and evidence gathered before dependencies formed. The International Longshore and Warehouse Union's technology clause did not prevent the introduction of port automation. It required advance notice, which created time for negotiation, which produced agreements that shared the gains rather than concentrating them. The mechanism is not friction for its own sake. It is friction applied at the right moment, when reversal is still possible, and alternatives remain.

We know how to hold institutions rather than individuals accountable for systemic failures. The 2008 financial crisis eventually led to capital requirements, stress tests, and living wills that imposed obligations on organisations that profit from risk rather than on the traders executing transactions. The framework is imperfect and contested, but it exists and can be extended. The principle that accountability must align with authority is not a new idea. It is a very old one, applied unevenly.

Sarah understood this. When she raised the issue of an early-stage nodule in her departmental meeting, she was told that the model's overall accuracy exceeded benchmarks. She stopped raising it, but she did not stop practising. What she needed was not better arguments. She needed an institutional structure through which her observation could be disseminated: a reporting mechanism, an independent audit, and a standard requiring the hospital to demonstrate that the system performed across the full distribution of cases rather than on average. Those mechanisms exist in aviation. They exist in pharmaceuticals. They do not yet exist at an adequate scale for diagnostic AI.

That is the work. Not resisting the technology, and not deferring to it. Building, in each domain where AI now makes the first move, the equivalent of what aviation built after the accidents of the 1970s: the conditions under which failure becomes visible before it becomes irreversible, under which accountability attaches to those with the power to change the system, and under which human judgement is not merely present in the loop but genuinely capable of stopping something when it needs to be stopped.

The violinist's software failed to capture the point. But the people who decided what a pharmaceutical company must demonstrate before approval did not miss it. The people who designed aviation's just culture did not miss it. The union negotiators who secured advance notice before automation did not miss it. They understood that the question was never whether the technology worked. It was whether the conditions under which it operated preserved what mattered.

We know how to do this. The knowledge is not the constraint. The will to apply it, before the window closes, is.

What We Build Next

The structures taking shape will determine whether human judgement remains necessary or becomes optional validation. That determination is shaped by decisions made now about governance, standards, and accountability.

The mechanisms already exist: professional bodies that require ongoing capability, regulatory frameworks that mandate review before deployment, procurement processes that demand transparency, labour organisations that secure consultation, and standards that preserve the conditions for autonomous thought to develop.

None of these mechanisms guarantee outcomes. They create space for questions to be asked, for evidence to be gathered, and for the gap between what technology promises and what it delivers to become apparent before dependencies lock in.

The question posed at the outset was: Who decides now? The answer is that decision-making authority has not disappeared. It has moved earlier in the sequence, where AI determines which options appear, which paths are viable, and what counts as reasonable before human judgement begins. We decide, but only from among the possibilities the system has already presented.

The evolving structures will determine whether human judgment remains vital or becomes only optional validation. That decision is not made at a single moment. Instead, it builds up over procurement procedures, regulatory frameworks, professional standards, and the small choices made by individuals who understand what is at stake and act accordingly.

The question is whether we will defend the conditions that allow us to question those possibilities. Whether human judgement remains necessary rather than optional. Whether decisions still belong to people even when they no longer begin with us. The window has not closed. The terms are still being written. The question is whether you will be in the room when they are set.

16

EPILOGUE FOR MANAGEMENT

Every generation of managers believes it is facing something entirely new, and almost always, the underlying pressures are familiar ones in new clothing. Metrics distort behaviour. Organisations grow around the tools they adopt until removing those tools would mean dismantling half the company. Competitors force each other into decisions no one would make in isolation. When things go wrong, the person who signed the form ends up answering for decisions shaped long before the form reached their desk. None of that began with AI.

What has changed is the way these pressures now move together. In many large firms, the same automated infrastructure screens job applicants, forecasts demand, sets price ranges, flags suspicious transactions, routes customer calls, and evaluates staff performance. The systems talk to each other through shared data and shared incentives, and they run all day, every day. A change in one corner, a tweak to a hiring model, a shift in demand forecasting or a new fraud threshold, ripples quietly into other decisions that no single team sees at once.

Automation itself is not new. Factory control systems adjusted machinery long before computers became common in offices. Aircraft have flown on autopilot for decades. Trading algorithms have bought and sold securities in milliseconds since the 1980s. What modern AI adds is reach. The same kinds of automated judgement now sit inside routine managerial work across departments that used to be separate. A credit officer opens a dashboard where applicants are already scored; a recruiter sees candidates ranked before reading a CV; a logistics planner works from forecasts that nobody on the team could reproduce by hand. The manager still decides, but the decision arrives half-made.

Once decisions begin that way, accountability becomes harder to locate. The credit officer signs off, yet the scoring model was trained on historical data chosen years earlier. The recruiter approves the shortlist, yet the ranking reflects features selected by engineers who never meet the applicants. The logistics planner adjusts stock levels, yet the forecast assumes demand patterns from a market that may no longer exist. None of these people are careless; they are working inside systems whose assumptions are easy to forget because they are invisible.

Measurement deepens the effect. Managers have always known that once a metric becomes a target, it stops measuring what mattered in the first place. The difference now is persistence. A call-centre team sees handling time updated minute by minute, a sales group tracks conversion rates in real time, a warehouse dashboard shows utilisation down to the hour. The numbers feel definitive, and the work that does not produce numbers fades from view. The senior engineer who remembers why a product failed five years ago looks less productive than the one closing tickets quickly, even though the first may be saving the company from repeating an expensive mistake.

Over time, the unmeasured work thins out. Teams stop documenting decisions because the documentation is not counted. Junior staff never learn the judgement their predecessors exercised because the system now does the first pass. Relationships with suppliers weaken because the procurement tool optimises solely for price. When conditions change, the organisation discovers that skills it assumed were unnecessary have quietly disappeared.

Dependency follows in ordinary ways. Companies that installed enterprise software in the 1990s rebuilt their processes around it and discovered later that replacing it would mean rewriting everything from payroll to purchasing. AI systems create similar lock-in, often faster, because they span multiple workflows simultaneously. Forecasting feeds staffing; staffing feeds customer service scores; customer service scores feed performance reviews; and those reviews influence who remains in the company long enough to notice problems. Each step looks sensible. The combination can be brittle.

Real examples show the pattern. Amazon abandoned an experimental hiring system after it learned to penalise CVs containing indicators associated with women because it had absorbed historical patterns from past hiring decisions. Dynamic pricing systems have raised prices during emergencies because they were optimising demand. Supply-chain software has reduced buffer stock in ways that left firms exposed when global shipping faltered. In each case, the software behaved as designed, and the damage came from assumptions that no longer matched reality.

When problems surface, organisations often search for the last person who touched the process. That instinct is understandable. It is also incomplete. Significant governance work is underway, including regulatory frameworks, model risk management rules, and audit standards across industries, but many firms are still discovering how widely automated decisions now reach. By the time an issue appears in a report, the chain of choices that shaped it may run through procurement teams, data engineering groups, vendors, and past restructurings, with no one person or group connecting them all in one place.

Consider a composite example drawn from several banks. A lending division automates small-business credit decisions, reduces staff in relationship roles and improves measurable efficiency. Months later, a regulator identifies a regional pattern in rejected loans that no one had noticed because dashboards tracked default rates and processing time rather than geography. The managers involved were competent. The models were updated regularly. Yet the staff who once spotted anomalies through conversation with customers were gone, and the system that replaced them had never been asked to look for that pattern.

Management has navigated earlier technological change, and it will do so again, but AI places strain on familiar practices because of how many decisions it touches at once. Hiring, pricing, logistics, risk management and customer support now share data and models in ways that blur the boundaries where oversight used to sit. Problems appear not because one system fails but because several systems, each behaving sensibly, interact in ways nobody anticipated.

There are practical responses. Firms can trace where automated scoring shapes decisions before a manager reviews them. They can track forms of work that current metrics miss, such as mentoring, cross-team coordination and memory of past failures. They can test optimisation goals against unlikely but plausible scenarios, maintain some human expertise even where automation works well, and align vendor contracts with the risks automation creates. None of this is new management theory; it is familiar practice applied earlier in the chain of decisions.

These steps will not remove the pressures described here. They will, however, make them visible sooner. The first sign that something is wrong should not be a regulator's question, a sudden customer backlash or a pattern nobody can reconstruct. If management can see how measurement, dependency, automation, and competition reinforce each other in ordinary work, it has a chance to adjust before the consequences arrive.

INITIATED BY AI

Notes on Sources

A. ACADEMIC JOURNAL ARTICLES

Arthur, W. Brian (1989). "Competing Technologies, Increasing Returns, and Lock-In by Historical Events." Economic Journal 99, no. 394: 116–131.

Autor, David H., David Dorn, and Gordon H. Hanson (2013). "The China Syndrome: Local Labor Market Effects of Import Competition in the United States." American Economic Review 103, no. 6: 2121–2168.

Bietti, Elettra (2020). "From ethics washing to ethics bashing: a view on tech ethics from within moral philosophy." Proceedings of the 2020 Conference on Fairness, Accountability, and Transparency, 549–559.

Brayne, Sarah (2017). "Big Data Surveillance: The Case of Policing." American Sociological Review 82, no. 5: 977–1008.

Burrell, Jenna (2016). "How the machine 'thinks': Understanding opacity in machine learning algorithms." Big Data & Society 3, no. 1.

Chen, Mark, Jerry Tworek, Heewoo Jun, et al. (2021). "Evaluating Large Language Models Trained on Code." arXiv:2107.03374.

Danaher, John (2016). "The Threat of Algocracy: Reality, Resistance and Accommodation." Philosophy & Technology 29, no. 3: 245–268.

David, Paul A. (1985). "Clio and the Economics of QWERTY." American Economic Review 75, no. 2: 332–337.

Elish, M.C. (2019). "Moral Crumple Zones: Cautionary Tales in Human-Robot Interaction." Engaging Science, Technology, and Society 5: 40–60.

Ericsson, K. Anders, Ralf Th. Krampe, and Clemens Tesch-Römer (1993). "The Role of Deliberate Practice in the Acquisition of Expert Performance." Psychological Review 100, no. 3: 363–406.

Gereffi, Gary, John Humphrey, and Timothy Sturgeon (2005). "The governance of global value chains." Review of International Political Economy 12, no. 1: 78–104.

Hagendorff, Thilo (2020). "The Ethics of AI Ethics: An Evaluation of Guidelines." Minds and Machines 30: 99–120.

Hardin, Garrett (1968). "The Tragedy of the Commons." Science 162, no. 3859: 1243–1248.

Helmreich, Robert L., Ashleigh C. Merritt, and John A. Wilhelm

(1999). "The Evolution of Crew Resource Management Training in Commercial Aviation." International Journal of Aviation Psychology 9, no. 1: 19–32.

Kitchin, Rob (2017). "Thinking critically about and researching algorithms." Information, Communication & Society 20, no. 1: 14–29.

Lum, Kristian, and William Isaac (2016). "To predict and serve?" Significance 13, no. 5: 14–19.

Mittelstadt, Brent (2019). "Principles alone cannot guarantee ethical AI." Nature Machine Intelligence 1: 501–507.

Obermeyer, Ziad, and Ezekiel J. Emanuel (2016). "Predicting the future: big data, machine learning, and clinical medicine." New England Journal of Medicine 375, no. 13: 1216–1219.

Rajpurkar, Pranav, et al. (2017). "CheXNet: Radiologist-Level Pneumonia Detection on Chest X-Rays with Deep Learning." arXiv:1711.05225.

Rapoport, Anatol, and Albert M. Chammah (1965). Prisoner's Dilemma: A Study in Conflict and Cooperation. Ann Arbor: University of Michigan Press. [Also listed under Books below]

Richardson, Rashida, Jason Schultz, and Kate Crawford (2019). "Dirty Data, Bad Predictions: How Civil Rights Violations Impact Police Data, Predictive Policing Systems, and Justice." New York University Law Review Online 94: 192–233.

Seaver, Nick (2017). "Algorithms as culture: Some tactics for the ethnographic study of algorithmic systems." Big Data & Society 4, no. 2.

Selbst, Andrew D., et al. (2019). "Fairness and Abstraction in Sociotechnical Systems." Proceedings of the Conference on Fairness, Accountability, and Transparency, 59–68.

Self, Will, and Seeta Peña Gangadharan (2019). "Understanding Audit Studies: A Framework for Policymakers and Researchers." Data & Society Research Institute.

Sherwin, Byron L. (2007). "Golems in the biotech century." Zygon 42, no. 1: 133–144.

Stigler, George J. (1971). "The Theory of Economic Regulation." The Bell Journal of Economics and Management Science 2, no. 1: 3–21.

Topol, Eric J. (2019). "High-performance medicine: the convergence of human and artificial intelligence." Nature Medicine 25: 44–56.

Tucker, A.W. (1950). "A Two-Person Dilemma." Stanford University. Reprinted in Readings in Games and Information, edited by Eric Rasmusen. Basil Blackwell, 1989.

Winner, Langdon (1980). "Do Artefacts Have Politics?" Daedalus 109, no. 1: 121–136.

Yala, Adam, Peter G. Mikhael, Fredrik Strand, Gigin Lin, Kevin

Smith, Yung-Liang Wan, Leslie Lamb, Kevin Hughes, Constance Lehman, and Regina Barzilay (2021). "Toward Robust Mammography-Based Models for Breast Cancer Risk." Science Translational Medicine 13, no. 578: eaba4373.

Yala, Adam, Peter G. Mikhael, Fredrik Strand, Gigin Lin, Siddharth Satuluru, Thomas Kim, Imon Banerjee, Judy Gichoya, Hari Trivedi, Constance D. Lehman, Kevin Hughes, et al. (2022). "Multi-Institutional Validation of a Mammography-Based Breast Cancer Risk Model." Journal of Clinical Oncology 40, no. 16: 1732–1740.

Yuan, Jing, Yu Zheng, Chengyang Zhang, et al. (2010). "T-drive: Driving directions based on taxi trajectories." In Proceedings of the 18th SIGSPATIAL International Conference on Advances in Geographic Information Systems, 99–108.

B. BOOKS

Abbott, Andrew (1988). The System of Professions: An Essay on the Division of Expert Labour. Chicago: University of Chicago Press.

Axelrod, Robert (1984). The Evolution of Cooperation. New York: Basic Books.

Baldwin, Richard (2016). The Great Convergence: Information Technology and the New Globalisation. Cambridge, MA: Harvard University Press.

Benjamin, Ruha (2019). Race After Technology: Abolitionist Tools for the New Jim Code. Cambridge: Polity.

Braverman, Harry (1974). Labour and Monopoly Capital: The Degradation of Work in the Twentieth Century. New York: Monthly Review Press.

Carpenter, Daniel, and David A. Moss, eds. (2014). Preventing Regulatory Capture: Special Interest Influence and How to Limit It. Cambridge: Cambridge University Press.

Carr, Nicholas (2014). The Glass Cage: How Our Computers Are Changing Us. New York: W.W. Norton.

Crawford, Kate (2021). Atlas of AI: Power, Politics, and the Planetary Costs of Artificial Intelligence. New Haven: Yale University Press.

David, Paul A. (1985). "Clio and the Economics of QWERTY." American Economic Review 75, no. 2: 332–337.

Dicken, Peter (2015). Global Shift: Mapping the Changing Contours of the World Economy. 7th ed. New York: The Guilford Press.

Dixit, Avinash K., and Barry J. Nalebuff (1991). Thinking Strategically: The Competitive Edge in Business, Politics, and Everyday Life. New York: W.W. Norton.

Ellul, Jacques (1964). The Technological Society. New York: Vintage. Translated by John Wilkinson.

Eubanks, Virginia (2018). Automating Inequality: How High-Tech Tools Profile, Police, and Punish the Poor. New York: St. Martin's Press.

Feenberg, Andrew (1999). Questioning Technology. London: Routledge.

Ferguson, Andrew Guthrie (2017). The Rise of Big Data Policing: Surveillance, Race, and the Future of Law Enforcement. New York: NYU Press.

Freeman, Richard B., and James L. Medoff (1984). What Do Unions Do? New York: Basic Books.

Gray, Mary L., and Siddharth Suri (2019). Ghost Work: How to Stop Silicon Valley from Building a New Global Underclass. Boston: Houghton Mifflin Harcourt.

Humble, Jez, and David Farley (2010). Continuous Delivery: Reliable Software Releases through Build, Test, and Deployment Automation. Boston: Addison-Wesley.

Kim, Gene, Jez Humble, Patrick Debois, and John Willis (2016). The DevOps Handbook: How to Create World-Class Agility, Reliability, and Security in Technology Organizations. Portland: IT Revolution Press.

Mahabharata, Drona Parva (Book 7). Translated by J.A.B. van Buitenen. University of Chicago Press, 1975. [Chakravyuha reference]

Mumford, Lewis (1934). Technics and Civilisation. New York: Harcourt, Brace.

Nader, Ralph (1965). Unsafe at Any Speed: The Designed-in Dangers of the American Automobile. New York: Grossman Publishers.

Noble, David F. (1984). Forces of Production: A Social History of Industrial Automation. New York: Alfred A. Knopf.

Noble, Safiya Umoja (2018). Algorithms of Oppression: How Search Engines Reinforce Racism. New York: NYU Press.

O'Neil, Cathy (2016). Weapons of Math Destruction: How Big Data Increases Inequality and Threatens Democracy. New York: Crown.

Osterman, Paul, Thomas A. Kochan, Richard M. Locke, and Michael J. Piore (2001). Working in America: A Blueprint for the New Labour Market. Cambridge, MA: MIT Press.

Ostrom, Elinor (1990). Governing the Commons: The Evolution of Institutions for Collective Action. Cambridge: Cambridge University Press.

Pasquale, Frank (2015). The Black Box Society: The Secret Algorithms That Control Money and Information. Cambridge, MA: Harvard University Press.

Rapoport, Anatol, and Albert M. Chammah (1965). Prisoner's Dilemma: A Study in Conflict and Cooperation. Ann Arbor:

University of Michigan Press.

Reason, James (1997). Managing the Risks of Organizational Accidents. Aldershot: Ashgate Publishing.

Ricardo, David (1817). On the Principles of Political Economy and Taxation. London: John Murray.

Rodrik, Dani (2011). The Globalisation Paradox: Democracy and the Future of the World Economy. New York: W.W. Norton.

Sassen, Saskia (2014). Expulsions: Brutality and Complexity in the Global Economy. Cambridge, MA: Harvard University Press.

Schelling, Thomas C. (1960). The Strategy of Conflict. Cambridge, MA: Harvard University Press.

Shortliffe, Edward H., and James J. Cimino, eds. (2006). Biomedical Informatics: Computer Applications in Health Care and Biomedicine. 3rd ed. New York: Springer.

Susskind, Richard, and Daniel Susskind (2015). The Future of the Professions: How Technology Will Transform the Work of Human Experts. Oxford: Oxford University Press.

Tsebelis, George (2002). Veto Players: How Political Institutions Work. Princeton: Princeton University Press.

Verbeek, Peter-Paul (2011). Moralising Technology: Understanding and Designing the Morality of Things. Chicago: University of Chicago Press.

Warsh, Cheryl Krasnick (2022). Frances Oldham Kelsey, the FDA, and the Battle against Thalidomide. New York: Oxford University Press.

Wiener, Norbert (1950). The Human Use of Human Beings: Cybernetics and Society. Boston: Houghton Mifflin.

Winner, Langdon (1980). "Do Artefacts Have Politics?" Daedalus 109, no. 1: 121–136.

Zuboff, Shoshana (1988). In the Age of the Smart Machine: The Future of Work and Power. New York: Basic Books.

Zuboff, Shoshana (2019). The Age of Surveillance Capitalism: The Fight for a Human Future at the New Frontier of Power. New York: PublicAffairs.

C. LEGAL AND REGULATORY DOCUMENTS

European Union (2016). General Data Protection Regulation (GDPR). Regulation (EU) 2016/679.

European Union (2024). AI Act. Regulation (EU) 2024/1689. [Referenced as 'A European regulation passed in 2024' regarding liability for AI systems in high-risk contexts.]

United States Congress (1962). Kefauver-Harris Drug Amendments to the Federal Food, Drug, and Cosmetic Act. Public Law 87-781, 87th Congress.

United States Congress (1966). National Traffic and Motor Vehicle Safety Act. Public Law 89-563, 89th Congress.

D. REPORTS AND INSTITUTIONAL DOCUMENTS

National Transportation Safety Board (2019). "Collision Between Vehicle Controlled by Developmental Automated Driving System and Pedestrian, Tempe, Arizona, 18th March 2018." Highway Accident Report NTSB/HAR-19/03.

E. NEWS AND MEDIA SOURCES

Hurricane Irma pricing (September 2017). Multiple news sources, including CNN, The New York Times, and CNBC. Coverage dated 6–10 September 2017.

F. LABOUR AGREEMENTS CITED

International Longshore and Warehouse Union. Pacific Coast Contract. - Technology clause referenced requiring advance notice before automation affecting jobs is deployed.

Works councils in Germany. General reference to consultation agreements required before major automation decisions. [No specific contract cited.]

G. FOLKLORE AND CLASSICAL TEXTS

The Golem legend. Jewish folklore. Used in the book as a metaphor for AI systems that continue executing instructions past the point of appropriateness.

The Chakravyuha formation. Hindu epic the Mahabharata, Drona Parva (Book 7). Used as a metaphor for AI lock-in dynamics. Translated by J.A.B. van Buitenen. University of Chicago Press, 1975.

H. FIELD OBSERVATIONS AND INFORMAL SOURCES

Rufous Treepie behaviour as tiger alarm. Field observations in Indian wildlife literature.

Honeyguide behaviour in northern Tanzania. Documented across multiple African cultures.

Amazon hiring system bias. Referenced as a documented real example. Drawn from public reporting.

Further Reading

Game Theory and Strategic Behaviour

Dixit, Avinash K., and Barry J. Nalebuff (1991). Thinking Strategically: The Competitive Edge in Business, Politics, and Everyday Life. New York: W.W. Norton.
An accessible introduction to game theory applied to competitive situations; illuminates the competitive dynamics described in Chapters 7 and 8.

Hardin, Garrett (1968). "The Tragedy of the Commons." Science 162, no. 3859: 1243–1248.
The classic article on how individually rational decisions produce collectively irrational outcomes. Directly relevant to the prisoner's dilemma of AI adoption.

Rapoport, Anatol, and Albert M. Chammah (1965). Prisoner's Dilemma: A Study in Conflict and Cooperation. Ann Arbor: University of Michigan Press.
The foundational text on the prisoner's dilemma; provides the theoretical basis for understanding why organisations cannot unilaterally slow AI deployment.

Technology, Work, and Professional Expertise

Susskind, Richard, and Daniel Susskind (2015). The Future of the Professions: How Technology Will Transform the Work of Human Experts. Oxford: Oxford University Press.
Examines how AI will reshape professions including law, medicine, education, and accountancy. Complements the book's treatment of Sarah and Marcus.

Zuboff, Shoshana (1988). In the Age of the Smart Machine: The Future of Work and Power. New York: Basic Books.
Prescient account of how computerisation transforms professional work and redistributes authority within organisations.

Globalisation and Economic Structure

Baldwin, Richard (2016). The Great Convergence: Information Technology and the New Globalisation. Cambridge, MA: Harvard University Press.
Explains how digital technology separated knowledge from proximity and transformed global supply chains; context for Chapter 4.

Rodrik, Dani (2011). The Globalisation Paradox: Democracy and the Future of the World Economy. New York: W.W. Norton.
Argues that markets, states, and democracy cannot all be simultaneously maximised; relevant to the governance questions in Chapters 13–15.

Sassen, Saskia (2014). Expulsions: Brutality and Complexity in the Global Economy. Cambridge, MA: Harvard University Press.
Analyses how complex systems produce brutal expulsions of people and communities; deepens understanding of the displacement described in Chapter 4.

Algorithmic Systems and Decision-Making

Burrell, Jenna (2016). "How the machine 'thinks': Understanding opacity in machine learning algorithms." Big Data & Society 3, no. 1.
Examines why machine learning systems are opaque even to their developers; relevant to the transparency and accountability arguments in Chapters 13 and 14.

Danaher, John (2016). "The Threat of Algocracy: Reality, Resistance and Accommodation." Philosophy & Technology 29, no. 3: 245–268.
Analyses the political implications of rule by algorithm; complements the 'right to think' arguments in Chapter 12.

Kitchin, Rob (2017). "Thinking critically about and researching algorithms." Information, Communication & Society 20, no. 1: 14–29.
Provides a framework for understanding how algorithms shape social life without determinism or technophobia.

AI Ethics and Governance

Bietti, Elettra (2020). "From ethics washing to ethics bashing." Proceedings of the 2020 Conference on Fairness, Accountability, and Transparency.
Critiques how AI ethics frameworks can serve as a substitute for real accountability; directly relevant to Chapter 14.

Hagendorff, Thilo (2020). "The Ethics of AI Ethics: An Evaluation of Guidelines." Minds and Machines 30: 99–120.
Reviews major AI ethics frameworks and identifies their limitations; useful background for governance discussions in Chapter 15.

Mittelstadt, Brent (2019). "Principles alone cannot guarantee ethical AI." Nature Machine Intelligence 1: 501–507.
Argues that ethical principles without enforcement mechanisms are insufficient; supports the book's emphasis on structural intervention.

Philosophy of Technology and Human Agency

Ellul, Jacques (1964). The Technological Society. New York: Vintage.
Argues that modern technique has become autonomous, subordinating human values to efficiency. A foundational text for the book's central thesis.

Feenberg, Andrew (1999). Questioning Technology. London: Routledge.
Offers a democratic theory of technology that resists both determinism and instrumentalism; suggests that technology can be redesigned.

Winner, Langdon (1980). "Do Artefacts Have Politics?" Daedalus 109, no. 1: 121–136.
Classic essay arguing that technologies embody political values in their design; essential context for understanding why AI systems are not neutral tools.

Verbeek, Peter-Paul (2011). Moralising Technology. Chicago: University of Chicago Press.
Examines how technology mediates human experience and shapes moral decisions; relevant to the 'right to think' arguments.

Historical Perspectives on Automation

Noble, David F. (1984). Forces of Production: A Social History of Industrial Automation. New York: Alfred A. Knopf.
Documents how automation decisions in the twentieth century were shaped by managerial control as much as efficiency; provides historical depth for Chapters 4 and 5.

Mumford, Lewis (1934). Technics and Civilisation. New York: Harcourt, Brace.
Traces the relationship between technology and civilisation from the clock to the machine; provides long historical perspective for the

book's argument.

Wiener, Norbert (1950). The Human Use of Human Beings. Boston: Houghton Mifflin.
  An early warning from the founder of cybernetics about the social consequences of automation; prescient and worth reading alongside this book.

Empirical Studies of AI Deployment

Elish, M.C. (2019). "Moral Crumple Zones: Cautionary Tales in Human-Robot Interaction." Engaging Science, Technology, and Society 5: 40–60.
  Analyses how accountability shifts onto human operators in human-machine systems when things go wrong; directly relevant to Chapter 14.

Gray, Mary L., and Siddharth Suri (2019). Ghost Work. Boston: Houghton Mifflin Harcourt.
  Documents the hidden human labour that enables AI systems to function; reveals the workforce behind the automation.

Seaver, Nick (2017). "Algorithms as culture." Big Data & Society 4, no. 2.
  Ethnographic approach to studying algorithmic systems in practice; challenges assumptions about how algorithms work in the wild.

Selbst, Andrew D., et al. (2019). "Fairness and Abstraction in

Sociotechnical Systems." Proceedings of the Conference on Fairness, Accountability, and Transparency.
  Argues that algorithmic fairness cannot be achieved through technical means alone; requires attention to social context.

Additional Works Recommended by Theme

On the erosion of professional expertise

Ericsson, K. Anders, Ralf Th. Krampe, and Clemens Tesch-Römer (1993). "The Role of Deliberate Practice in the Acquisition of Expert Performance." Psychological Review 100, no. 3: 363–406.
  The foundational research on how expertise develops through deliberate practice; essential reading alongside Chapter 11's argument about skill maintenance.

Carr, Nicholas (2014). The Glass Cage: How Our Computers Are Changing Us. New York: W.W. Norton.
  Examines how automation atrophies human skills and judgement across numerous domains, with vivid case studies from aviation, medicine, and design.

On algorithmic discrimination

O'Neil, Cathy (2016). Weapons of Math Destruction. New York: Crown.
  Accessible account of how big data algorithms amplify inequality

in hiring, education, criminal justice, and finance.

Eubanks, Virginia (2018). Automating Inequality. New York: St. Martin's Press.
Documents how automated systems harm vulnerable communities, with particular attention to welfare and housing.

Noble, Safiya Umoja (2018). Algorithms of Oppression. New York: NYU Press.
Examines how search engines perpetuate racial stereotypes and discriminatory outcomes.

Benjamin, Ruha (2019). Race After Technology. Cambridge: Polity.
Analyses how 'race-neutral' technologies often encode and amplify racial hierarchies.

On surveillance capitalism

Zuboff, Shoshana (2019). The Age of Surveillance Capitalism. New York: PublicAffairs.
Comprehensive account of how digital platforms extract and commodify human behavioural data; relevant to the book's discussion of AI-mediated attention.

Crawford, Kate (2021). Atlas of AI. New Haven: Yale University Press.
Examines the material and political costs of AI infrastructure, from mines to data centres to labour.

Pasquale, Frank (2015). The Black Box Society. Cambridge, MA: Harvard University Press.

INDEX

A
Abhimanyu, 59
accountability, 109–118
    distributed responsibility, 114–115
    gap, 110–111
    oversight as theatre, 111–112
    speed problem, 112–113
    where it must land, 117–118
AI Act (EU, 2024), 116–117
AI systems, as first movers, 12–14, 15–24
Aisha Salem (character), iii–iv, 30–31, 60, 64, 73–74, 79, 107
algorithmic trading, 61, 70, 111–112, 133
Amazon hiring system, 135
artificial intelligence
    see AI systems
atrophy, cognitive, 85, 96–97
automation
    compared with offshoring, 39–40
    dependency on
        see dependence
    historical context, 35–38, 133
    labour becomes optional, 39–40
aviation regulation, 128–130

B
bias, algorithmic, 23–24, 113–114, 135

C
Chakravyuha, 59–60
cognitive capability, 82–89, 91–98
    atrophy, 85, 96–97
    deliberate difficulty, 86–87
    maintaining under pressure, 85–87
cognitive liberty, 91–98
collective action, 105–106
competitive dynamics, 61–62, 69–74
    competitive spiral, 61–62
    prisoners of progress, 69–74
context blindness, 47–53
    airline pricing, Hurricane Irma, 49–50
    just-in-time supply chains, 50–51
    predictive policing, 51–52
cooperation trap, 57–58
CT scans
    see diagnostic AI; radiology

D
decision-making, relocated, 15–24
deliberate practice, 83–89, 91–98
dependence
    as trap, 58–59
    cognitive, 85–87
    reversal difficulty, 32–34, 41–45
diagnostic AI, 3–8, 27–28, 31–33, 41, 77–78, 83–84
    mammography (Mirai model), 3–7
    overlay system, 1–3, 8–10
discharge summaries, AI-generated, 20
distribution, as personal strategy, 78–81

E
economic structure, 35–40, 55–56, 69–74
education, thought experiment, 91–92
efficiency metrics
    see measurement; throughput
elsewhere, age of, 35–40
emergent outcomes, 113–114
expertise
    connective tissue, 27–28
    experience gates, 30–31
    manufactured scarcity, 29–30
    relational positioning, 25–34

F
financial markets
    see algorithmic trading
first move, AI's, 1–14
framing, 21, 91–92

G
GDPR (General Data Protection Regulation), 104–105
Golem legend, 47–48, 52–53
governance, 126–131
    aviation, 128
    automotive safety (Nader), 126–127

INDEX

pharmaceutical (Kelsey/thalidomide), 127–128
GPS navigation, 18

H
healthcare
 see *diagnostic AI; radiology*
hiring algorithms, 10–11, 23, 113
 Amazon example, 135
 experience gates, 30–31
hinge (chapter), 75–76
honeyguide bird, ii
Hurricane Irma pricing, 49–50

I
influence, structures of, 99–108
institutional lock-in
 see *lock-in*
International Longshore and Warehouse Union, 102, 129

J
just-in-time supply chains, 50–51
Justin (character), 62

K
Kefauver-Harris Amendment (1962), 127–128
Kelsey, Frances, 127–128

L
labour
 becomes optional, 39–40
 offshoring, 36–38
 unions, 63, 101–102
ladders, employment, 38–40
legal accountability
 see *accountability*
liability, 115–116, 115–117
lock-in
 cost of removal, 32–33, 41–45
 dependency, 58–59
 structural, 75–76
logistics depot, 19, 41–43, 101

M
mammography AI (Mirai), 3–7
management, epilogue for, 133–137
Marcus Tropos (character), iii–iv, 25–34, 34–40, 43, 55–65, 73, 79–81, 85, 87–88, 107, 117
measurement
 as frame, 19–24, 44–45
 signal vs noise, 21–23
 throughput metrics, 8, 27–28
Mirai mammography model, 3–7

N
Nader, Ralph, 126–127
National Traffic and Motor Vehicle Safety Act (1966), 127

O
offshoring, 36–38
overlay, diagnostic
 see *diagnostic AI*

P
pandemic, supply chain impact, 50–51
PACS (Picture Archiving and Communication System), 2
predictive policing, 51–52
prisoners of progress, 69–74
procurement processes, 99–100
professional standards, 102–103

R
radiology
 see *diagnostic AI*
ranked before seen, 23–24
recommendation algorithms, i–ii, 16–18, 94–95
redundancy, 25–26, 55–56, 81
regulatory capture, 103–104
relational positioning, 25–34
reversal difficulty
 see *lock-in; dependence*
right to think, 91–98
Rufous Treepie, ii

S
safety, autonomous vehicles, 109–110, 118

INDEX

Sarah Patel (character), ii–iv, 1–14, 22–23, 27–28, 31–33, 40, 41, 52, 59, 63–64, 73, 75, 77–78, 81, 83–84, 85–86, 100, 105–106, 107, 111, 117, 120
scarcity, manufactured, 29–30
signal and noise, 21–23
supermarket loyalty app, 16–18
supply chains, 50–51, 135

T

Tempe, Arizona (autonomous vehicle death), 109–110, 118
thalidomide, 127–128
throughput metrics
  see measurement
transparency, 104–105
traps, 55–67
  cooperation trap, 57–58
  dependence trap, 58–59

U

unions
  see labour, unions

V

veto points, 100–101
violinist, thought experiment, 119–120

W

warehouse
  see logistics depot
what remains human, 119–132
works councils, Germany, 102, 129

www.ingramcontent.com/pod-product-compliance
Lightning Source LLC
Chambersburg PA
CBHW020658220526
45464CB00001B/487